MW01102163

1992

THE AFTERTHOUGHT

THE AFTERTHOUGHT

West coast ROCK Posters & Recollections
from the '60s BY JERRY KRUZ

RMB

please return to Hendrik Beune
hendrikbeune@gmail.com
mobile Vancouver 604-499-5452

Contents

please return to Hendrik Beune

hendrixbeune@gmail.com

Acknowledgements

There are so many people to thank in the creation of this book, so many who helped in so many ways. I am sure I will forget to mention someone, so I am apologizing in advance to anyone I've left out.

First and foremost I thank my wife, Julie, for without her there would be no book. Also our children and their mates: Celeste and Dale Low, Damian Kruz and Angela Miranda, and Justine Kruz and Patrick Doyle. And our grandchildren: Riley, Gabe, Tyesa, Ethan, Julian, Liam, Corrigan, Blair and Rosie and nephew Chris. And of course, I would also like to commemorate my mother, Mary Kruz (1910–2002).

I am indebted to Patrick Doyle, who stepped up to the plate when I needed someone to do interviews. Also to Eric Wilson, an author in his own right, who, along with his wife, Flo, gave me the confidence that I could write a book.

Thanks are also due to Grace Gorman, who believed this could be a great book, and to RMB publisher Don Gorman, editor Joe Wilderson and art director Chyla Cardinal, who saw it through to print.

And of course to the wonderful artists who created the posters: Doug Cuthbert, Bruce Dowad, Bob Masse and the late Frank Lewis; and to all the band members and light show people who performed at the Afterthought!

I would further like to thank Dr. Anton (Tom) Kolstee, Richard (Dick) Cruickshank, Mike Trew, Jeff Ridley, Renee Dupree (Rick Enns), Rocket Norton, Terry Kruz,* Henry Kruz,* Les Vogt, Tom Northcott, Allan Garr, Dan McLeod, Sam Perry,* Mike Mitchell, Wayne G., Danny Kennedy,* Jon York,* Jessie Kerr, Joanne Rocco, Ron Ulmer, Lynn Brooks,* Arlene Mason, Greg Evans, Gary Anderson, Aaron Gordon,* Dal Grauer,* Sonny Hancock, Annette Humphries, Joe Astopovich, Jeffrey Barnett, Peter Barnett, David Barnett, Paul Deyong, Mia Lewis, Matt Laundrie, Pam (Tim) Burge, Gary "Chicken" Hirsh, Country Joe McDonald, Ann Mortifee, Paul Horn,* Adrian Chamberlain, Ed Chell, Tommy Chong, Mike Devlin, Lloyd Smith,* Bill Doig, Theresa "Bitty" Neel, Sam Feldman, Bruce Allen, Norman Gidney, Michael Velletta, Roger Schiffer,* Red Robinson, David Lemieux, Paul Martein, Lloyd McKinnon,* Bill Finlayson, Gil Henry, Jamie Hirsh, Howie Vickers, Danny Tripper,* Yvonne Vanheddegem, Bonnie Kramer, Peter Hodgson (Island Graphics), John Shields, Gerry Riley, Doug Hawthorne,* John Tanner, Jerry Lucky, Dr. Stephen Roome, Dr. Samaad Malik, Pam Renney, Winnie Jeffery, Lee Clippingdale, Diane Johnson, Nina Lyons, Bill Seavey, Penny Barner, James Shepard, John Shepard, Tom Shepard,* Dennis Vance, Walter Laurer, Ken Webber, Lon Wood, Gary Vanbusker, Dimitri Demers, Nick Blasko, Larry and Sheila Snider, Bill McElroy, Richard Mulcaster, Mike Kyer, Glenda MacMillan, Don Bellamy and Jennifer Ansen.

(* indicates people now departed.)

1

Introduction, Posters and Recollections

"Critical mass," was my son Damian's remark when I told him that the date of the first event I ever promoted – November 6, 1965 – was the same date Bill Graham, my mentor and the eventual owner of the Fillmore Auditorium in San Francisco, put on his first event, a benefit for the San Francisco Mime Troupe. Chet Helms, the manager of the Avalon Ballroom, also did one at about that time. I believe these dates taken together were the start of what is known as the psychedelic era.

The beginning of my career was quite different from Graham's or Helms's, though. Unlike them, I didn't start out wanting to be a promoter. I wanted to be a priest. Being the youngest in my family, this was expected of me and I'd always believed it was to be my life path. Despite coming from an extremely dysfunctional and abusive family, I had been able to survive my childhood largely because I was blessed with an incredibly supportive and liberated mother, Mary Kruz, who somehow managed to guide me through my childhood.

In early adolescence I was introduced to assorted drugs and of course alcohol. My school attendance was less than stellar, as was my learning. What a great start to young adulthood.

When an opportunity arose to do a road trip across Canada with my best friend, Wayne G. (on a 50 cc Honda step-through motorbike!), I took it. When we came upon St. Vladimir's, a minor seminary in Roblin, Manitoba, the visit was the catalyst that made me finally decide to pursue a calling to the priesthood. I began at St. Vladimir's in September of 1965.

I remember so clearly driving to St. Vladimir's from Winnipeg with a cousin of mine. On the way, a song came on the radio: "Pretty Woman," by Roy Orbison. As it played I started to wonder, "What am I doing?" All I could think of as the song played was Julie, my true love. I should have realized it was a sign from above. Even my cousin Bill Zbrosky, who worked for CBC TV, was asking if I really knew what I was doing. Clearly I did not.

After a very short attempt at the seminary, I returned to Vancouver to my first and only love. Not knowing what to do next, I accompanied Julie to her youth group at St. John's Anglican church. She introduced me to the priest who had started the group, Rev. Eric Powell. He was looking for a way to engage teens and felt that a good way to do this would be to start a coffeehouse. When he asked me if I would help, my first response was "Why me?" I soon realized he had confused me with my older brother, Terry, whom he had met on a canoe trip in northern BC and had heard perform as a folksinger. Eventually I agreed, though, for I had been attending local coffeehouses for a number of years already and I figured I could do this. How hard could it be? It seemed like a good idea, and that was my start as a promoter.

NOVEMBER 6, 1965: ST. JOHN'S CHURCH HALL

COFFEEHOUSE FEATURING AL & DIANE

Since I had no experience with promotion, and no idea of what I wanted to with my life, I figured I had nothing to lose. Allan Garr, a friend of my brother's who had arrived in Vancouver with two girls in a Volkswagen and spent many evenings at my mother's eating dinner, was pursuing a career as a student at Simon Fraser University and was also a folksinger. It seemed to me that everyone wanted be a folksinger and/or guitarist. My brother was willing to help anyone attain this goal, and that included Allan. When I approached Allan to do this gig, he was more than willing and said he had met Diane Kehoe, who, you guessed it, was also a singer. What a great name for a group: Al & Diane. I now needed a name for the coffeehouse, so I asked Julie to help me think of one. She came up with the Afterthought, which was the title of a poem from her Grade 12 English course. Now all I needed was a poster. Allan had a friend who was attending art school and agreed to do a poster using a linocut technique. Little did I know this would be the first of many posters to come. We then promoted the event, and yes, it was successful!

Poster 1 ➤

NOVEMBER 20, 1965: ST. JOHN'S CHURCH HALL

COFFEEHOUSE FEATURING JOHN LOME

What to do next? The first event had been successful and the youth group wanted more. Rev. Eric also agreed that it should continue, so what else to do but plan for the next coffeehouse? Since this was my first time planning another event, two weeks seemed like plenty of time to find an act and advertise.

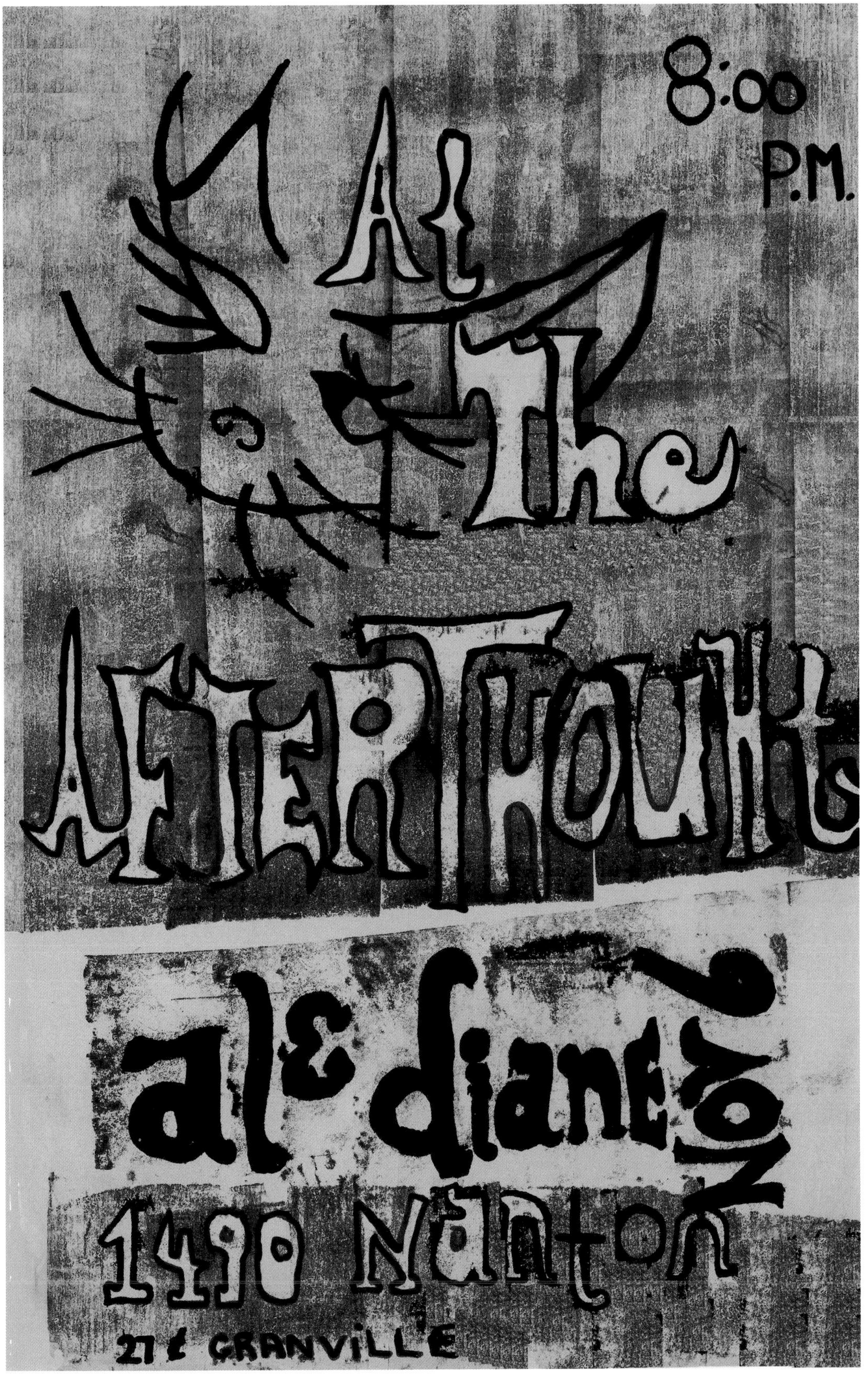
8:00 P.M.
At The
AfterThought
1490 Nanton
GRANVILLE

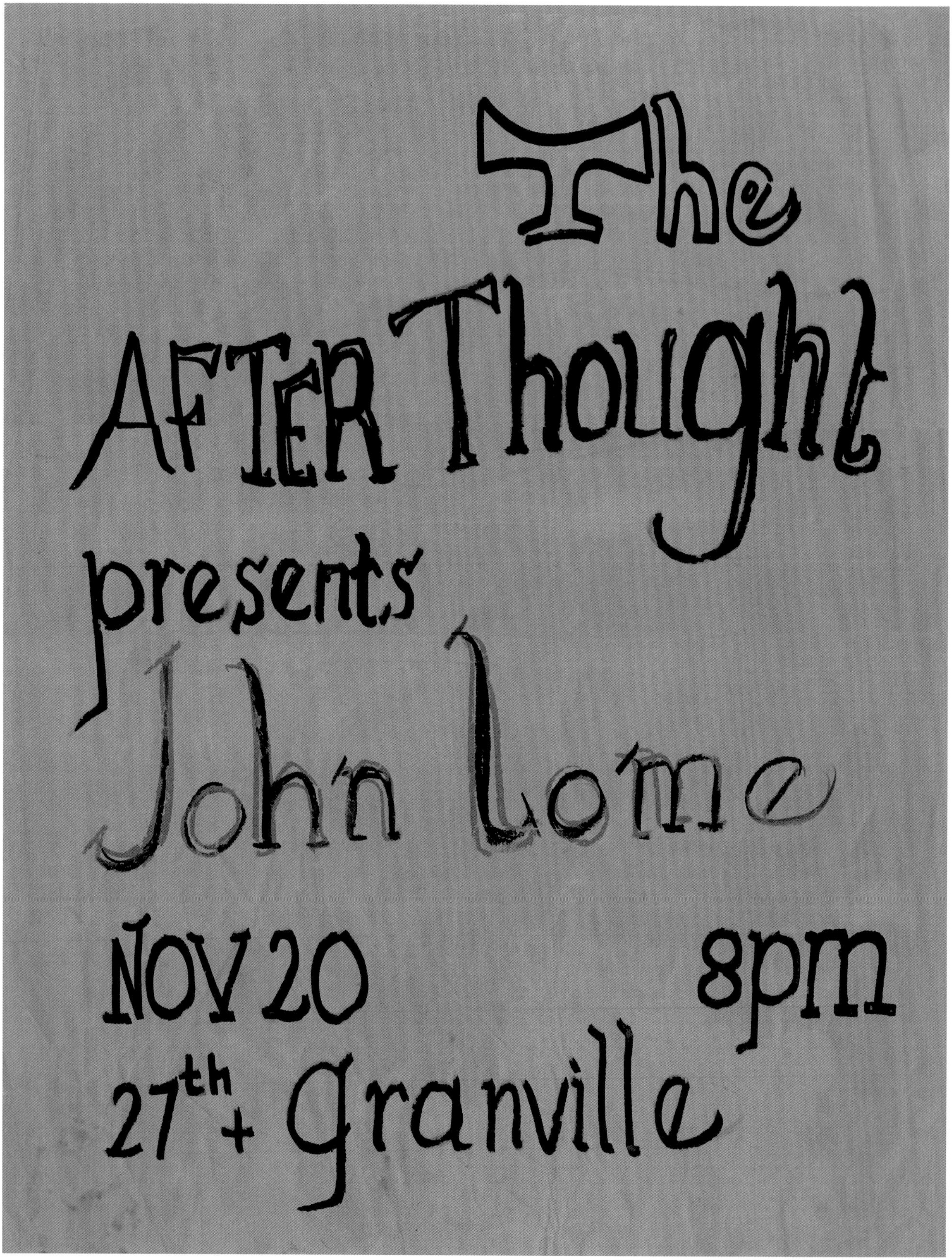
The
AFTER Thought
presents
John Lome
NOV 20
8pm
27th + Granville

But where to find another new act?

Allan had been a big success and he was a Toronto transplant. And what do you know – my brother had another friend from Toronto who was also a great folk singer with an original sound: John Lome. Only much later did I learn that his original sound was really from Fred Neil, who was performing a New York knock-off. You can't blame Lome for trying, though, and besides, this was pre-Internet and he could get away with calling it an original sound.

◄ *Poster 2*

This was when I learned that the west and east of Canada might as well be two different worlds. Even with the different times of today I'm not sure the east coast and the west coast are not still different worlds. Maybe some things never change. After John Lome convinced me he would be the best act I could possibly get, I agreed to hire him. However, I then told him he had to make his own poster and I would need at least half a dozen copies. As you see, he did this great poster on kraft paper. You could say every copy was an original, too, as each one had to be hand-drawn.

JANUARY 20, 1966: ST. JOHN'S CHURCH HALL

COFFEEHOUSE FEATURING TOM NORTHCOTT TRIO

What to do next? The two coffeehouses were successful events and the youth were happy, but now they wanted a bigger band. Meeting with Rev. Eric, we agreed it would be good to continue with the coffeehouse. However, it was now getting close to Christmas and there would be a lot of other events coming up at the church. Taking this into consideration, it was agreed we would start up again in the New Year. Little did I know how 1966 would be a milestone year that would change my life.

So now what? Christmas would be upon us before we knew it. It was pretty simple: I had to find a way to make some money. What I was discovering was that I could convince people as to what they wanted. I later learned that this was known as marketing. Who knew?!

Bringing up this subject makes me remember an incident from when I was around 10 years old. My school had a contest to see who could sell the most raffle tickets. I won the first prize, $5, which was a lot of money to me then. I discovered that near the school were buildings with secretarial pools in them, and that I could sell tickets to most of the people working there. In other words, selling to groups as opposed to one customer at a time. This was probably the most valuable information I learned in elementary school.

So what could I do to make some money? My best friend, Wayne G., came up with the idea to open up a Christmas tree lot. He had somehow figured out that he could cut fir trees from under the power line up the Sunshine Coast for free. What could go wrong with free trees? Next we needed to sell them. It turned out that my friend Allan Garr, from Al & Diane, had an empty lot next to his house which nothing was being done with. It was on a major street in Vancouver, Fourth Avenue, which was at that time Vancouver's answer to Haight Street in San Francisco. We made our plan: Wayne would cut the trees and I would sell them. What could be easier than that,

and we would split the profits. To this day Wayne still thinks it was not fair, because he did all the manual work and all I had to do was sell. A lot was learned from this experience as to the power of marketing!

It was now the start of a new year and a new coffeehouse. There was an up-and-coming local folksinger by the name of Tom Northcott, whom I had met on the coffee house circuit. Tom had a great idea to try singing as a trio, which I thought might work, and this was the start of the Tom Northcott Trio. When it came to asking Tom to supply his own poster, though, his answer was a flat no. But since my father owned a local printing shop, it was simple: I would go there and design and print what I needed. This was my first self-designed poster and also printed by me. The event went off without any problems, except the youth all said they wanted more rock and roll and less folk music.

Poster 3 ➤

FEBRUARY 18, 1966: ST. JOHN'S CHURCH HALL

NIGHT TRAIN REVUE

We had now completed three successful coffeehouses, but the youth were already tired of them. Three had been enough. They wanted something different: they

the afterthought
27 th & Granville Street

Presents

TOM NORTHCOTT TRIO!

Friday January 28 th.
Doors Open 9:00 p.m.

wanted good old rock and roll. We needed a meeting with Rev. Eric to discuss what direction to go in. Eric agreed we could hold a dance in the large gym located in the church hall. Great idea, why not? So what that I had no experience in putting on a dance. I hadn't had any experience putting on coffeehouses and I pulled that off, so why not a dance?

So how do you find a rock band if all you know is folk music? The Yellow Pages of course (remember those?). It turned out that in Vancouver in 1966, if you looked up "Rock and Roll," you found Jaguar Enterprises, operated by Les Vogt. Les, I later found out, had been a somewhat famous rocker himself whose band had opened for Bill Haley & The Comets when they played Vancouver in the early sixties. I phoned and Les invited me to his office. We hit it off immediately. At that time I didn't know that we would become life-long friends. Les introduced me to his roster by showing me the glossy 8 × 10 photos of all his assorted bands. I tried to at least sound like I knew what I was doing. Finally we agreed on a very large R&B band called the Night Train Revue, the farthest thing from folk music one could imagine. And this time I didn't even ask if the band would supply their own poster.

After confirming the date with Rev. Eric, I went straight to my father's print shop to make one myself.

For the next while I prayed everything would work. The word was out that there was going to be a big dance at St. John's church hall. The information moved out beyond the youth group, into the local schools and kids at large. By this time of course, I was getting very, very nervous about what I was getting into. The night of the dance my brother told me he had the answer to my nervous state: magic pills. To this day I am not sure what he gave me, but I do know that whatever it was, it knocked me out until the early evening. Somehow I made it to the dance to find kids trying to climb through the basement windows to gain entry, as the gym was packed and church staff had stopped letting any more people in. It was a great success and enjoyed by everyone, excluding the adults who attended, of course. They were not happy. It turned out that the elders of the church had said "no more!"

I realized that this could be a great business opportunity. I could hold the next one on my own. Or could I?

Poster 4 ➤

the afterthought
27th & Granville Street
Presents: **Big Band R.B.**

NIGHT
TRAIN
REVUE

Friday, Feb. 18th
Doors Open 8:30 p.m.

MARCH 11, 1966: SCOTTISH AUDITORIUM

THE CENTAURS

What should I do? The St. John's church elders had had enough, but the kids were having too much fun; they all wanted me to put on another dance. So the question became "How do I do it?" I thought back to my early teens attending coffee houses and meeting their owners. (See the story at poster 7, page 18.) I realized that this was a business opportunity, not only to have fun but also to make money, which I had none of.

First I had to find a venue, so back to the Yellow Pages, the Internet of the time. The Scottish Auditorium, at 12th and Fir, seemed to fit. It was a great location, close to where the last dance had been, so the St. John's youth group could find it by taking the bus or whatever. I knew they could figure it out. One big problem: I had no money. I figured out that the thing to do was to open a bank account. I am 17 years old; it's time I should have my own bank account. The Scottish Society, who owned the hall, agreed to accept a postdated cheque.

Next I had to find a band, so back to Les Vogt who had supplied me with the Night Train Revue. Out of his large roster of bands, Les told me about a great group called the Centaurs. They too agreed to a postdated cheque.

Now I needed a poster. So back to my father's print shop, where I designed and printed some, and with a lot of help from my friends we put them up everywhere. Now pray that "the youth" will come!

I was very nervous when the big night arrived, March 11, 1966, just three weeks since the last dance. However, this one was all on my own. Youth arrive and start buying tickets and they just keep coming. Before I know it, the hall is full (plus a few extra!).

Wow, my first solo event is a success! I put the proceeds into the bank on Monday morning. There was enough to cover the cheques I had written, with money left over. I had learned how to make money and do something I liked. What a feeling. It's easy to put on a dance. My roller coaster ride had begun!

Poster 5 ➤

the afterthought
Presents:
THE CENTAURS
Friday, March 11 th.
12th. & Fir.
Doors Open 8:30 p.m.

APRIL 7, 1966: PENDER AUDITORIUM

TOM NORTHCOTT TRIO

So here I go. I need a bigger hall, as the last two events had been packed to the rafters. Back to the Yellow Pages and I find the Pender Auditorium, a hall located in downtown Vancouver that will hold a thousand. The number seemed overwhelming. I had two successful dances behind me and everyone wanted to help, with a whole lot of new ideas to make it bigger and better. I am standing in the middle of this great hall being overwhelmed and wondering how I am going to fill this. I've booked the venue for April 7, which does not give me a lot of time to do everything. Out of nowhere this young adult comes up to me and introduces himself. Says his name is Sam Perry and that he can put on a light show for me that will keep time with the music being played and will be projected onto the walls of the venue. What a concept! This had not been seen in Vancouver before. We agreed to do a light show with the band. (Unfortunately, Sam would later become the first of many casualties in this very dangerous business. For more about his work, see the website *Ruins in Process: Vancouver Art in the Sixties* listed in the Related Reading and Viewing section.)

Now to find a band. Just at this time, folksinger Tom Northcott comes to me and says he has gone electric but I would need to get a second band, as he did not have enough material to perform a whole show. No problem! One of my best friends from elementary school, Tom Kolstee, had formed a band in the last few months. They called themselves the Molesters and they had been performing at local house parties. I thought I could use this band as the second on the bill, but they would need to change their name. After much discussion, Tom, the lead guitarist, came up with the name United Empire Loyalists.

I knew I needed a really good poster, a better one than I could do myself. I approached my friend Frank Lewis, who I believed was one of the best illustrators around. The poster, I would soon learn, is the most important part of promoting an event. I am still not sure how I got him to agree to do one for this show, but he did.

The poster was made with Letraset, a system that enabled the designer to place letters separately on the artwork and had

Poster 6 (as printed) ➤

TOM NORTHCOTT TRIO

ARTY/MUSI/OPTI/HAPPENING
SAM PERRY

ALSO THE UNITED EMPIRE LOYALISTS

PENDER AUDITORIUM/APRIL 7

AT 9:00 P.M. AT 339 W. PENDER

other design elements you could add such as flowers. This poster would prove controversial in that the establishment felt it was promoting the use of drugs etc. because the flowers looked like they were coming out of Tom's head.

I now had to promote this like no other! While I was doing that, someone asked me if I had a licence. "What licence?" I asked. "A business licence, of course." "Well, where do I get that?" "City Hall," they said. So, next stop Vancouver City Hall. But first a stop at home to put on a suit, because I have also learned that you have to be over 18 years of age to attend a dance hall (a very old law on the books). This could be a big problem for me because I am only 17 and will not be 18 until May 15. I apply for the licence, pay the fee and receive the document. Fortunately they never asked me for ID.

Now I am told I have to have security, so back to the Yellow Pages. Guard dogs, that's the ticket. Who is going to argue with a German shepherd? No one at all, I would soon find out.

The night of the dance, all is good. I am very nervous, but the event was nevertheless a big success. I had pulled it off again. Wow! I did not know it at the time but I believe this was the first dance "happening" of its kind, and that it helped in part to pave the way for the psychedelic movement on the West Coast.

Poster 6a (original artwork) ➤

THE 21ST BIRTHDAY BASH AT THE MANSION: A TRIBUTE TO DAL GRAUER

I am not sure exactly when Dal Grauer, a friend of my brother's, became a very good friend and supporter of mine. One of my first recollections is of Dal asking if I would help him plan his 21st birthday party. He wanted a band to play at his house, and invited me over. When I arrive there, I see it's not just a house but a very large mansion. I drive through the gates and park in the circle driveway and Dal takes me to the lower level into what appears to be a virtual ballroom, which he refers to as his recreation room. We get down to planning, and of course the band I suggest to him is the United Empire Loyalists, whom I happen to be managing by this time. The party is to take place right after my first dance at the Pender Auditorium.

On the appointed day, we arrive at the mansion and set up the band, the lights and everything else, and the party begins. What I observed that was different about this event – besides the luxurious mansion, of course – was that there was a high

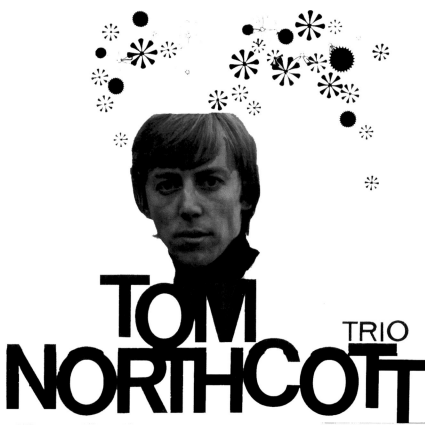

TOM NORTHCOTT TRIO

ARTY MUSI OPTI HAPPENING
SAM PERRY

ALSO THE UNITED EMPIRE LOYALISTS

PENDER AUDITORIUM APRIL 7

level of security at the gates. I remember going out to chat with the security guys and being told that part of their job was to make sure the police would not disturb the party.

The evening went off without a hitch and a good time was had by all. This would be the first time I would plan an event other than a dance.

I feel very fortunate to be able to say Dal was good friend over the years; we would have many good times together. Less fortunately, though, we both rode the drug roller coaster in our youth, through a lot of crazy times. I spent a lot of time just chilling at his house. I remember one such day at the house when I was drinking a martini with Dal, and his mother came in to chat. She told me she was impressed with what I had done, but said I could do so much more and I had great potential. She offered to pay for my education if I went back to school and on to university. I very quickly said no, thank you. Little did I know that I would have so much more to learn and how painful it could be.

I wanted to share this tribute to Dal, a great man, father and grandfather and someone I was proud to call a friend. It was during my research for this book that I learned of Dal's passing on August 31, 2010. Rest in peace, my friend.

COFFEEHOUSES AT THE BUNKHOUSE

MOSAIC, THE INQUISITION AND THE QUESTION MARK

Sitting reflecting on a flight to San Diego with Julie for a reunion of our entire family, which now totals seventeen, I realize how fortunate I am to have survived and to have such a fantastic family. Julie had always said that if she were ever able to bring the entire family together for a reunion she would do so. Due to an inheritance from her Aunt Rina it became possible.

Our youngest daughter, Justine, is married to Patrick Doyle and living near Ottawa with their three children, Corrigan, Blair and Rosie, and Patrick's son Liam, who lives in Toronto. Our son, Damian, with his wife, Angela, and their three children, Tyesa, Ethan and Julian, live in Victoria. Our eldest, Celeste, and her husband, Dale, along

Poster 7 (Bunkhouse menu) ➤

THE BUNKHOUSE MENU

FOLK MUSIC NIGHTLY

612 DAVIE ST
•VAN•
B.C.
683 9790

PIZZA
CHEESE..........100
MUSHROOM......135
SALAMI.........135
PEPPERONI......135
COMBINATION...150

ICE CREAM
DRUNKARD.....40
SCREWBALL....65
BABYS BOTTOM 25
A VIRGIN.......65
A STUPID DUPER $100

DELUXE SANDWICHES
A LITTLE PIGGY
ham on rye with garnish

A FOLKS WHEELER
salmi on rye with garnish

STORKS DELIGHT
corn beef on rye with garnish

POOR' BOY
ham cheese salami and corn beef with garnish

CHEESE STRUM
cheese with garnish
HOT 95¢ COLD 85¢

??? OH BOY ???
HOT 65¢ COLD 65¢

DRINKS
COKE...........25
ORANGE.........25
SPRITE.........25
FRUIT PUNCH....45
"BUNKHOUSE CIDER" 45
SWAMP WATER....45
ICE ESPRESSO...45
FLOATS.........45

HOT DRINKS
CANADIAN COFFEE....20
TEA................20
HOT CHOCOLATE......25
CIMMERIAN..........25

PASTRY
FRENCH PASTRY
AND
APPLE STRUDEL
25¢ EACH

with their two children, Riley and Gabriel, reside in San Francisco. For over a week I was able to watch our eight grandchildren just be children, and to observe and enjoy along with their parents. This was the first time for all of us to be together. One could see and feel they were all family. This week was incredible; as they say, there was love in the air. This was also during the time I was writing this book. It made me realize what I had missed in my own youth yet somehow survived. I was unable to tell my family why at times I was having so much trouble just coping. Memories can do strange things.

In the early sixties there was a large coffeehouse movement throughout North America. We were known as beatniks, of which I'm sure I was the youngest in Vancouver. I was about 12 when my education in coffeehouse culture started. Though I was underage, I had the benefit of my older brother working at various coffeehouses, so I was able to attend. I was told the same thing by all the club owners: sit in the back, be quiet and watch. I did this for several years. I now realize this experience prepared me to pull off the first of a series of psychedelic dances. Who knew that coffeehouses would be the start my informal education?!

From as early as I can remember, my childhood and youth were difficult and filled with abuse. The coffeehouses became my safe zone. The downside of this was the start of my use of a lot of assorted drugs. I would come to realize there would be a big price to pay for this informal education, but I am grateful and feel extremely blessed to have survived. As I look at all my family I realize that it was sure wonderful that I had a soulmate who was willing to wait for me, and most important stand by me as I went on the drug roller coaster and so many adventures in operating a psychedelic dance hall. It was Julie who made sure I would survive!

MAY 8, 1966: PENDER AUDITORIUM

UNITED EMPIRE LOYALISTS AND THE BITTER SWEETS

Could I do it again? It seems all of my friends think I could, and I did need an income. Could this be my career? My limited education seemed to point me in this direction. City Hall had given me a licence for a year, even though I was still too young to attend my own dance hall. All of this must mean I could succeed at this.

Poster 8 ➤

presents

2

the afterthought

UNITED EMPIRE LOYALISTS

PLUS *the*

BITTER SWEETS

GREAT BANDS

PENDER AUD MAY 6th

DOORS OPEN 8:30 P.M.

PLUS

WECO HAPPENING

ADVANCE TICKET SALES POT SHOP 1420 W PENDER

The Pender Auditorium was owned by the Boilermakers Union, and at the time, it was in fact their union hall. They were willing to rent it to me any time they were not using it for one of their functions. It was a great space with an equally great history. The hall was on the second floor, with a grand staircase leading up to it. Before you walked into the hall proper there was a foyer that was a great space for a concession, which I would soon learn generated great cash flow. The Turkish Delight chocolate bar would become the bestseller (too long a story to tell right now). Right across from the entrance to the hall there was a great mural of the history of the Boilermakers Union. On the opposite wall, above the entrance, was a balcony that ran the length of the hall. That was where Sam Perry would show me how to set up all the light show equipment to project images onto the opposite wall. The mural was a problem, but Sam said it was an easy fix to just cover it up with white bedsheets.

Now that we had the hall and light show all figured out, we had to get busy planning the event. First step had to be the bands. The United Empire Loyalists of course wanted to play (they would soon become my house band). But there was a problem, in that, like Tom Northcott

earlier, they did not have enough material to perform a whole set. Back to my friend Les Vogt to find another band. Les tells me he is starting to get more acts in his stable that are psychedelic, and that a great new one is the Bitter Sweets. A deal was made and my lineup was complete.

Next, the light show. After the first one with Sam Perry I discovered there were many people that worked on these shows besides Sam. The name Light Show was changed to weco Happening. When Sam expressed his dislike of the name change, I thought nothing of it and brushed off what he was saying. This would prove to be the beginning of my learning about people skills and compassion, skills I would need for the rest of my life!

Now for the next task: the poster. After the numerous complaints I received about the last poster being too suggestive, I decided to be more traditional and use the "boxing style" I was more familiar with, but spice it up with pink and print it using the silkscreen method instead of using my father's shop. Can you tell that although I am making money now, I still have a lot to learn about people's feelings?

Finally everything was ready and the event was another great success. My head gets even more swollen!

MAY 20, 1966: PENDER AUDITORIUM

THE CENTAURS

I had now put on seven events. Each one had been bigger than the last and I think I have developed a system that works. I am still only 17, but come May 15 I will finally be of legal age to attend my own dance hall.

One of the first things I did way back in my first dance at the Pender was to establish a good security system to both keep the underage kids out and of course keep the peace inside. The guard dog services were working, as no-one would pick a fight with a dog, a German shepherd no less, and its handler. The company convinced me to increase security by having two dogs and handlers, one at the entrance and one at the back exit.

So let's get on with putting on another event. The Afterthought is the talk of the city, or at least so I believed, and that was all that mattered at the time. Of course, in such a short period of time I had developed a large ego, even though I did not even know what an "ego" was. It seemed that everyone wanted a dance as soon as possible. This time Les Vogt is phoning me, telling me that the Centaurs, the first group I booked on my own, were going on a European tour. I thought they must

be great if they were going to perform internationally. It was this line from Les that convinced me to book them even though I had to pay them more money.

I also believe it was Les who told me he knew of a great poster designer by the name of Doug Cuthbert, who by chance was also the drummer for the Night Train Revue, the first band I ever booked. Doug would be the first graphic artist I would hire to design a poster. I made it clear in our oral contract that I retained all rights to the poster design.

The very first artist to design a poster for the Afterthought, of course, was Frank Lewis, but somehow I did not think of him as merely a commercial artist. I considered him as my brother then and I still do. At the time, though, I had no idea how our lives would continue to play out together. When I first met Frank, I was 15 and he was 29. I commissioned him to do a portrait of my grandparents for my mother. It was a gift I was very proud to give her, and she too would later play an important part in the dance hall.

Mom passed at age 92, having lived long enough to meet her first two great-grandchildren. She would be so proud to know there are now eight of them. The painting of my grandparents now hangs proudly in my home, waiting to be passed to the next generation.

As a side note, my now 10-year-old granddaughter Riley, who lives in San Francisco, asked me what I was doing when she saw me writing this. When I told her, she replied, "Are you trying to become famous?" Children are always so very honest, and it took me a very long time to figure out that by far my best accomplishments in life are our three – Celeste, now 43; Damian, 39; and Justine, 35 – together with their respective spouses, and of course my own lifelong soulmate, Julie, and our grandchildren. By the end of this book you will find out how I came to this realization.

Another profound grandkid thought, this one from 8-year-old Gabriel: "The older you get, grandpa, the harder it gets to understand what kids do." It's hard now to comprehend how, way back then, I believed that if you were over 30 you couldn't be trusted! I would eventually learn just how profound Bob Dylan was back in 1964 with that line in "My Back Pages" that

goes: "Ah, but I was so much older then / I'm younger than that now."

Finally everything is in place and I feel I can pull this one off in two weeks. The date is set for May 20, 1966, five days after my 18th birthday. Everything goes as planned and I make a lot of money. I think I am on top of the world! But I have so much to learn.

Poster 9 (original artwork) ▲
Poster 9a (as printed) ➤

the afterthought presents

THE CENTAURS

Doors
8:30
OPTIONAL
DRESS and
TRIP
to
all
over 18
PLUS

WE:CO
HAPPENING

PENDER AUDITORIUM
339 PENDER ST. MAY 20

JUNE 3, 1966: PENDER AUDITORIUM

UNITED EMPIRE LOYALISTS AND THE JABBERWOCK

There is buzz in the city about what I am doing, and it seems everyone is coming to me with a new idea of what I can do to make the dances bigger and better!

The person that seems to have the most ideas is my older brother, Terry, now 21. I am nervous about his input, though, because five years earlier, when I was only 13, he had introduced me to the pleasures of alcohol, cannabis and an assortment of pills, many of which to this day I do not know what they were. Terry was a very accomplished folksinger and guitarist, but I never really gave him a chance. I always thought I knew more than he did. Yet he was the one who introduced me to the people I needed to know to become a successful promoter, including Vancouver *Province* columnist Jack Moore. I never thanked Terry once for anything positive he did for me, and it took me until I started to write this book to realize how insensitive I had been to my friends and family all along. Something else I did not know about was that by this time Terry was addicted to heroin. He had told me

he'd played with all the drugs that were out there, but he claimed he had it under control. I never really gave it any thought other than to notice that he looked stoned all the time. It would be many years later that I would lose my brother to a heroin overdose. I will always wonder what would have happened if I had intervened in some way that he would still be here with us.

So again I have only two weeks to put it together. The date would be June 3, 1966. Of course I would use the United Empire Loyalists, because I was their manager (see Figure 14 opposite page 37 for the UEL business card and membership card designed by Frank Lewis). The Loyalists were rapidly becoming the band to be seen in the city. Up until now most of the groups had been pretty conservative, which was not what I was looking for.

Then along comes John Cluff, brother to Robert, who was a childhood friend of my girlfriend, Julie. John says his band's name is Jabberwock, from *Alice in Wonderland*, and that they are willing to play. The band would later change their name to

Poster 10 (original artwork; no printed poster) ➤

My Indole Ring. For reasons I still cannot understand, I said the band was from Toronto. I must admit I figured it looked good to bill a band as being from out of town. Doug Cuthbert produced a great poster. I had him include the words "optional trip & dress" with a line through "trip &." This was the start of my getting more and more stoned a lot of the time. In spite of my drug input, though, the dance went off without a hitch and more money was to be had. I believed I was on a roll and nothing could go wrong.

I am very fortunate to have a core of childhood friends who I would later learn became my lifesavers. They were Danny Kennedy, Anton "Tom" Kolstee and Wayne G. We had become friends in Grades 2 and 3 at St. Augustine Catholic school. When I was 15 Wayne had talked us into attending a party in Shaughnessy, an upwardly mobile neighbourhood on Vancouver's west side where Wayne's family had moved. It was at this party that I first met Julia Biden, who would become my soulmate and wife. So my foursome became a fivesome. None of us knew at the time that I was at the start of a very dangerous roller coaster ride. Thank God for good friends who always had my back.

JUNE 17, 1966: PENDER AUDITORIUM

BANDS UNKNOWN

It's time for the next happening. I know that's what I called them because of the following article written by Jack Moore under the name "Keith Leslie." My brother, Terry, had set up this article, as Jack was another personal friend of his.

So what happens when an 18-year-old gets a full-page story in a leading daily newspaper such as Vancouver's *The Province*? The article talks about how great this guy is and calls him an "impresario,"

even if he himself had to look up the word in the dictionary. He gets what is commonly known as a swelled head, or more commonly a very large ego. What could go wrong? Even the newspaper said I was successful. Therefore it must be true. I had lots of money, girls chasing me (I later

[Figure 11]
(Vancouver Province *clipping; original event poster missing)* ➤

It's happening here, there and everywhere

By Keith Leslie

A happening, by definition, used to be something that wasn't planned. It just sort of — well, it just sort of happened.

Recently, however, a Vancouver group called Afterthought Productions has been planning happenings very carefully, and throwing them for an unusual bunch of young folk.

And, strange as it may seem, these happenings are happening too.

So what's a happening?

Well, by Afterthought's definition, it's a sort of teen-age dance in overdrive, with special optical effects thrown in.

While a band, usually a large one, plays teen music at ear-splitting volume (which seems to be the only way the teeners can hear it), a group of people armed with slide and motion picture projectors cast strange images on the walls, ceiling, floor and the dancers themselves.

The images often move in time with the music, sometimes out of time with it, and sometimes they revolve slowly, giving some of the participants the impression they are dancing on the wall.

Pretty soon the whole thing gets to the kids, and they get to doing a lot of free-form dancing, sometimes without a partner in sight.

"This," says 18-year-old impresario Jerry Kruz, "is when things start happening."

Kruz, with his brother Terry and a strange man named Sam Perry who organizes the projection equipment and staff, runs these dances. And so far, after six of them, they're turning a healthy profit.

"The secret of the whole thing," bellowed Kruz over the sound of the band, "is to get the right kind of kids to come. You don't see these kids at other dances."

Indeed you don't. There were teenagers in red suits and flowered shirts, ballet slippers and bare feet, and a wild combination of mod clothing and what-have-you.

"These kids are cerebral, they dig new things," howled Kruz. "We just don't have any trouble with them.

"We put on strange new things for them to appreciate, and they appreciate them. It's that simple."

They certainly seemed to be having a good time, all right. Come intermission, when everyone (well, everyone over, say, 21) was just about ready to clutch ears and run screaming down the street, the with-it-kids just sat down on the floor of the Pender Auditorium, where these things are thrown, and listened to recordings of Tibetan chants and electronic music, at a volume lower than that of the band.

Over by the inevitable soft-drink counter, with its bewildered girl cashier, a bunch of the kids were talking about Canadian theatre, and the possibilities of catching this year's Stratford festival.

(Remember what the dances were like when we were in school? I think we used to talk mostly about automobiles and girls and movies and girls and girls.)

"We just seem to appeal to the right bunch of kids," Kruz bellowed after the music had started again. "In 10 years, these people will be creating things. They'll be the ones who are coming up with the new ideas in the arts. Mind you, we also have a group of older (in their twenties, yet) people who are already doing things.

"This is the group that will be happening. Now they're gathering ideas, assimilating, learning. Wow."

Kruz, who gets awfully excited when he talks about these young people, started the whole idea a few months back when he put on a church dance.

"I'd heard about this thing being done in the States, but at that time it had only been done at private parties. So I gathered up Sam Perry and his projection equipment and tried it. It worked."

From there, he said, it was a short step to renting a hall and trying the idea out on a larger group.

That worked, too. He's been holding these op hops every two weeks.

"Next, I plan to go weekly. But I'm a little afraid of that. See, we don't know yet how much the traffic will bear. Maybe they only want these dances one every two weeks."

"It's kinda hard on the eyes and ears if you do it too often," I said, but nobody heard me.

Fascinating op art patterns were playing on the dancers, and wild old medieval woodcuts and drawings were being swished from side to side on the far wall. A film clip that looked like oil on a rain puddle ran over and over in eerie color while the dancers leaped and whirled and rocked and stood nearly still, as the fancy took them.

Kruz says if the idea really catches on, he will open a club for them.

"In a club, we could design the projection stuff to cover the whole room, whereas in a large hall we can only get most of it.

"Of course, we'll have to make sure it's profitable first."

Seems to be, so far. Kruz estimates he gets between 500 and 700 youngsters out to these bashes.

"We can't charge too much, though. They have no bread, so we have to keep the price down."

They didn't look particularly poverty-stricken, although judging by the males in the crowd, there are a lot of barbers going hungry.

Along about 1 a.m. the optical effect got hypnotic, and some of those on the floor developed that vacant-eyed catatonic look. Kruz himself got out on the floor and the whole thing took on the air of a religious rite.

We more senior citizens leaned against the wall while the lights spun around us, and gradually engulfed us along with the dancers.

Far off in a corner, Spotlight photographer Dave Paterson looked at his light meter and began to cry, ever so softly.

discovered they were called groupies). Thank God I had my close circle of friends attempting to keep me grounded. Julie, of course, had the most difficult job, because we knew we were in love. The problem was I had no idea at the time how to handle this thing called love. All I thought it was about was "sex, drugs and rock and roll."

That too had to be right, although the song that made that phrase famous wouldn't come out until ten years later.

Anyway, the dance is great, and I am told the story will be out by June 30, which is the date of the next dance, as I had to take the July 1 long weekend into account.

JUNE 30, 1966: PENDER AUDITORIUM

TOM NORTHCOTT TRIO

Tom Northcott tells me he and his band now have enough material to do a whole show without needing a backup act. One band, more money for me. What else could I want? I really thought I was on top of the world. This happening came together quite easily and the attendance was huge. How could it not be, considering that on the day of the happening I had a full page story in *The Province*!

Time for a little reflection about where I'd gotten to so far. One of the regulars at my dances, Lyn, was a draft dodger who had driven his brand new yellow convertible up from California. He could no longer afford the payments on the car and did not want to get traced to Vancouver, so we agreed on a price and I took over his payments. I am

18 years old, driving a 1965 Mustang convertible, which I believed was the hottest car in town. Pow! as the poster puts it.

At the same time, with a group from UBC that I thought were the elite, I'd started experimenting with a new drug, LSD, which was legal at the time, not that that made any difference. My brother was cohabiting with two wonderful ladies who were regulars at the dance hall. Only problem was, they did not know Terry was living with both of them at the same time. Come to think of it, nobody knew, except Terry, of course. One of the ladies, Glenda MacMillan, offered to take me on a guided

Poster 12

(original artwork; no printed poster) ➤

POW

Tom Northcott Trio

ThURS

JUNE 30 8:30 PM

AFTERTHOUGHT • 339 PENDER

RESTRICTED!!!! 18 YRS. AND OVER

'REBEL'
(NOT RIEL-LY)

HEY! PLUS WECO HAPPENING

tour of a book called the *Tibetan Book of the Dead*. This was the book Timothy Leary allegedly read to go on a journey of the mind using LSD as a portal instead of the years of praying and studying that the Tibetans do to attain enlightenment. How could a kid say no to such a deal? Everything was set. I swallowed the LSD tab and lay down beside Glenda with my head on her lap. I embarked on the most amazing journey. At one point I experienced leaving my body, which I could see clearly as I gazed down on it. Then it was time to travel with my spirit. I ended up I believe with my brother on the other side of town, where I watched him with Jennifer Anson, the other girl he was living

with at the time. Then I came back to my body and Glenda. What a trip!

After this first trip I went on to drop a lot more acid. I was foolish enough to believe I had transcended to another level of consciousness. What is really scary is there were a whole lot of other people who also believed it. I will have many more reflections about this as we travel through these posters of my life. I want to take the time to say, to any young people reading this book: please understand, there was nothing cool about what I did. I thank God I survived and am able to write about my life. For the ones who were there, let it be a memory that we survived, and let us not forget the ones that did not.

Terry and Glenda ➤

JULY 8, 1966: PENDER AUDITORIUM

THE BITTER SWEETS

Ten concerts completed and I was getting ready to put on number eleven. Since the full-page newspaper story came out I've been receiving a lot more attention. It seems everyone wants to help me. Although it did make me wonder why, I was very naïve in not thinking there may have been some financial motive for the help offered. Les Vogt was offering me a new up-and-coming band called the Bitter Sweets. He also offered to rent me an office at Jaguar Enterprises, his company. I thought it was great deal; I now had not only a band for July 8, but an office too!

I am at the office when along comes a gentleman by the name of Harry Ornest. He introduces himself and tells me he is running something at the Pacific National Exhibition called the Teenage Fair. He explains that it is a fair within the fair, with an event called a battle of the bands, and has bands playing all day and evening. He asks me if I would like to look after this at the fair. For compensation he will pay me $100 a day plus expenses and a parking space in the PNE grounds very close to the Teenage Fair. My answer was a very fast yes. I thought I had died and gone to

heaven. What a great deal! An interesting aside is that I learned forty years later (from Les, who to this day remains a good friend) that Les had been doing this job in previous years and had been paid twice what I was getting. It seems Harry wanted somebody younger for the job who could relate to the teens better. Since I was in fact still a teen myself, it was a perfect match.

Of course I again needed a poster. Bruce Dowad was the bass guitarist for the United Empire Loyalists at the time and trying hard to become an illustrator. He asked if he could create a poster and I thought why not. It seems all is in order: I have a new job, an office, and everything is set. I am feeling a little overwhelmed, but everything is cool.

As I said, I am getting approached by many different people, all wanting to be my partner, all telling me how they can make the Afterthought even better and of course make me more money. I sure have a lot to learn. Nevertheless I take on the first of my three partners. This one, Dennis Vance, would turn out to be the best. I realize now that he was most interested in the ladies he could link up with at the hall.

THE AFTERTHOUGHT PRESENTS
ANOTHER HAPPENNING WITH THE

BITTER SWEETS

339 W PENDER JULY 8 RESTRICTED TO 18yr. +over

ADDITIONAL INFORMATION AT POSITIVELY FOURTH STREET

But he also had a business I thought was cool: he sold pottery out of a small Pender Street storefront right in front of his house. It was called the Pot Shop, and of course I figured it would be a great ticket outlet for the dance hall.

◀ *Poster 13*

JULY 22, 1966: PENDER AUDITORIUM

UNITED EMPIRE LOYALISTS

How much can change literally overnight! The Afterthought was all the buzz and the Friday night thing to do for the youth of the city. Up until now there hadn't been anything much for them besides movies, school dances and drive-ins. That was about to change, big time.

It turned out that Sam Perry and some others, who at the time were being referred to as the "left of centre" group, had been working for quite awhile to put on something called the Trips Festival. While all of us may have been cast by the establishment as "hippies" and there were many fringe types within our group, I felt the Trips Festival was pretty much the same thing I had been doing, only a hell of a lot bigger. Instead of two bands, there would be six. The light show would be huge, not just on one wall but on all the walls. The venue, the Garden Auditorium, was four times the size of the Pender, where my dance happenings took place.

The night of my dance finally arrived, but all week the energy and vibes had not been good. Attendance, which up to now had been increasing every time, was down. I confronted Sam as to why he was doing this to me, as I took things very personally. Sam said he thought he could do it better than me and he would do so. He invited me to the Trips Festival the following week to see for myself. Since that was an off weekend, I figured I'd best go check it out and size up what I believed to be my first competition. I did not know it at the time, but this was only the beginning of much change in the entertainment business for youth in Vancouver and all of North America.

United Empire Loyalists
MEMBERSHIP CARD

738-8826

THE
UNiTED
EMPiRE
LOYALiS TS

manager:
JERRY KRUZ

◄ *[Figure 14]*
(Loyalists membership card and business card; no poster available)

JULY 29–31, 1966 TRIPS FESTIVAL: GARDEN AUDITORIUM

GRATEFUL DEAD, BIG BROTHER & THE HOLDING COMPANY, JEFFERSON AIRPLANE

So off I go to check out the new competition on the block, with my sweetheart Julie and the United Empire Loyalists. I am not sure what to expect. We arrive at this very large hall and of course I walk in like I own the place. What I see first is lights everywhere: strobe lights, disco balls, all of it pulsating to the music. I must admit I was impressed. At least I think I was. It would be many years before I would discover what a big financial disaster this event was. The bands, the organizers, the financial person, no one was happy. And again, it is important to note that I did not learn about this until after I was out of the business.

I scout out the venue and then go backstage and talk to the bands they have booked from San Francisco. First I meet the Jefferson Airplane. Grace Slick and Marty Balin are having some kind of dispute and I am not impressed. I tell myself that they won't make it. Next, Big Brother & The Holding Company. I see Janis Joplin sitting by herself. She seems very lonely. I introduce myself and she extends an invitation to come visit her in San Francisco. Why not; I thought it would be fun. Next up, the Grateful Dead. I see Jerry Garcia and introduce myself. I am very impressed and think to myself that this band has something happening. Out of nowhere comes an idea (to this day I don't know where it came from): I ask Jerry if he wants to perform at my dance hall the following week. He says he would love to and we agree on a fee of $500 plus accommodations and I think probably expenses. We shake hands and my first deal with an American band is done. This $500 fee would become the benchmark for all our out-of-town bands. Julie and I stayed and enjoyed ourselves, but I knew I had to come up with accommodations for the band before the Trips Festival was over.

Next day, what to do? Where do you put up the Grateful Dead for a week, and what should it cost? I talk it over with my dad. He and I don't get along all that well but he is a commercial printer and lots of his customers are hotel owners. He tells me of a customer with a motel on Kingsway, one of the main routes into Vancouver. I go over there and meet the owner and explain to him what I need. He shows me a very large room with a lot of beds in it. How many beds I was not sure but it looks good to me and reminds me of the dormitory at St. Vladimir's, the minor seminary I attended before I became a rock promoter. How quickly one's life can change. I make the deal and I now have accommodations for the band.

I meet the Dead after the festival and take them to their digs for the next week. I pack as many of them into my car as will fit and have the rest of them follow us to the motel. I have a chance to talk with Jerry, as he is sitting in the front seat of my hot car. I find him to be a great guy and he tells me they have been staying at a crash pad since they arrived, so whatever I have will be better. I park the car, get the room keys and show the band the large single room in the basement (I would rather think of it as ground level). The band all let it show that they are not impressed. Then, what I perceived as a very large man comes up to me and introduces himself as Owsley. He tells me he is the band's manager and that the accommodations are not good enough and the fee I am paying the band is not acceptable. I tell him too bad, I made my deal with Jerry Garcia and as far as I was concerned it was Jerry's band. Only later would I learn that Owsley Stanley was a somewhat infamous LSD manufacturer and dealer who would also become a pioneer concert audio guy. Who knew?

Poster 15 ➤

AUGUST 5, 1966

GRATEFUL DEAD

I have hired the Grateful Dead to perform at the Afterthought and now I need a poster. Bruce Dowad of the United Empire Loyalists had done my previous poster, and I believe he also did this one. Unfortunately, this one couldn't be found.

electric TRIPS media FESTIVAL

JULY 29 30 31
FRI·SAT·SUN
PNE GARDEN AUDITORIUM

After over forty years we tracked Bruce down in Hollywood, California, where he now lives with his family, and met for lunch. After he left the band, Bruce had gone on to art school and developed an international career in commercials and film. He agreed he had done the poster just before this one and also the following one, so we concluded he must have done the one for the Grateful Dead as well. The poster seen here is a recreation of the original to the best of our and Bruce's knowledge. It was printed two-up on 8½ × 11 stock, a smaller size which I thought would be easier to distribute and cheaper to print, even though I was printing at my father's shop and it wasn't costing me anything.

Poster 16 ➤

AUGUST 1–5, 1966: HEYWOOD BANDSTAND ON BEACH AVENUE GOING INTO STANLEY PARK

COMMEMORATIVE POSTERS: GRATEFUL DEAD FIRST FREE CONCERT

So, what do you do when you've told Jerry Garcia you will show him and his band a good time while they are waiting to perform in your dance hall? The show is August 5 and today is August 1. (Many years later I found out that Jerry's birthday was August 1.) First thing: introduce them to the band that will open for them, namely the United Empire Loyalists, whom I happen to manage. The musicians meet one another and seem to hit it off. Jerry Garcia and Tom Kolstee appear to connect right from the start. I noticed as the week went on that Garcia took on a mentoring role with Tom, and it was really cool to observe how things unfolded.

After a couple of days of sightseeing and hijinks with the local band, the Dead want to rehearse. UEL drummer Richard Cruickshank says no problem, use my house; my parents are out of town. This would be the time to point out that the ages of the Loyalists ranged from 16 to all of 17. I had just turned 18, but most of the members of the local bands were still under 18, so it was not legal for them to attend the dance hall either. The legal drinking age was 21, and the age to be classified as an adult was 18. So off we all go to Richard's house for some rehearsal. Somehow the word got out in town that the Grateful Dead were practising at Richard's house. Surprise, surprise, the practice turns into an out of control party. Next thing we know, the neighbours have called the police and things get really out of hand.

I forget to mention that Richard's parents' house was in a very wealthy part of the city with a great view of Stanley Park, the ocean and downtown Vancouver. [A more in-depth account of this evening can be found in Darren Gawle's United Empire Loyalists interviews cited in Related Reading.] Richard had wonderful parents, but I don't believe they ever forgave any of us for that crazy night.

Well here it is Wednesday, August 3, and I am giving the Dead a tour of the city. The buzz just seems to be getting bigger and bigger. Jerry, of course, is riding with me in my Mustang with the top down. How cool is that? We are driving along Beach Avenue when Garcia sees a gazebo bandstand across the street from the beach on the way to the entrance to Stanley Park. Jerry says stop the car, he wants to check out the gazebo with the rest of the band. He then tells me – does not ask me – just says he wants to do a free concert at the gazebo. I ask what he means and he asks me if I want the dance this weekend to be success. Sure, of course. Well, then, everybody has to know about it, he says, and what better way to tell them than a free show?

Next thing I am doing is finding out how to get the keys to the gazebo and permission to do a free show. The keys were easy, the lifeguard at the beach across the street agrees to open up the electrical, and the next thing I know the band is in the gazebo setting up. To this day I am not sure how it all came together. I do know that I did not get permission from the city and it did not take long for the police to shut the whole thing down. Julie and her parents were trying to drive through the area that day but could not because of the traffic jam this event caused.

Footnote: it would not be until forty-plus years later while doing research for this book that I found information online about the "Lost Dead Concert." I found out that, short as it was, this was the first free Dead concert ever. [See "Grateful Dead First Free Concert" under Related Reading and Viewing.]

So, here we are on Thursday, one day before the concert, and I have been told by Jeff Ridley of the United Empire Loyalists that another attempt was made to do a concert at Kits Beach which may or may not have occurred. I have no memory of this. The only recollection around this is taking pictures of the Dead posing on the old train that was at Kits Beach. Truth be told, I have very little memory of that week. It would appear I was in an altered state of consciousness for most of the time. What a surprise.

The posters you see here are a recent creation for the free concert. They are intended to be commemorative and were designed by Gary Anderson of Turntable Records, located in Fan Tan Alley in downtown Victoria, BC. Gary has been selling Afterthought posters, vintage records and posters from all over the world for the past 25 years. It is a great shop to visit!

Poster 17 ➤

AFTERTHOUGHT Presents

THE
GRATEFUL DEAD

FREE

CONCERT

Gazebo at First Beach Park
West End, Vancouver, BC
Wed. August 3rd, 1966

AFTERTHOUGHT Presents

THE GRATEFUL DEAD

FREE
CONCERT

Gazebo at First Beach Park
West End, Vancouver, BC
Wed. August 3rd, 1966

AUGUST 5, 1966: PENDER AUDITORIUM

GRATEFUL DEAD AND UNITED EMPIRE LOYALISTS

I am writing the story of a very important night with the Grateful Dead for the second time. Unlike life, you can get a second chance to do it again. After much searching as to what I'd initially written, it was simple: I pushed the undo button. (Up until then I did not know there was an undo button on my computer. I definitely know now! Wouldn't it be nice if life were that easy?) As I reflect on what I just wrote and now have the benefit of doing again, after telling Julie what I had just done, it does make me realize how much has happened in my real life that did not have the benefit of a do-over.

We started the afternoon of August 5 setting up the sound rig. I had never seen so much equipment before! It just seemed to keep coming and coming. This stuff was different from any other band gear I had ever seen. It was custom-developed by Owsley "Bear" Stanley, who was the Dead's audio designer and financier as well their manager. Owsley was very particular about everything being just right. After several sound checks, all was ready for what I believe was the best concert I have

◄ *Poster 18a (commemorative)*

ever seen. This was a show like no other. There were 1,000-plus patrons and the hall was hopping even before the bands started. The United Empire Loyalists opened. I could tell how much Garcia had already influenced Tom Kolstee in his week of mentoring. Garcia's playing style would affect Kolstee's for the rest of Tom's career.

Now the Dead mount the stage, and shortly after they start the entire room starts to move to the music like waves in the ocean. Owsley is walking through the room dispensing acid to anyone who opens their mouth. This of course results in a very high-energy crowd. The evening ends at midnight with the Dead playing Wilson Pickett's *In the Midnight Hour*. The patrons are going wild. The police arrive and say, "Jerry, you know you are supposed to be shut down by midnight!" I tell the police to follow me up into the hall. They see the entire room vibrating en masse, pulsating to both the Dead and the light show. It is truly a sight to behold. The police turn and look at me and say, "Alright, shut it down when the band finishes their set." The night finished without any trouble; absolutely nothing went wrong that evening. But this would be the last time I would ever see the Vancouver police be so co-operative.

Now, to the poster. The version on the previous page is a commemorative one, as noted earlier. But let me tell you the back story about what happened. In 1992 Bob Masse came to visit at our house. I was very glad to see him, an old friend from my past. I was not in very good health at the time, having just completed a year of treatment for hepatitis C. As my loving wife pointed out to me, did I not expect there would eventually be some payback for my wild youth? I agreed and indeed was grateful to be alive. So, from those days, of course, Bob wants to see the original Afterthought posters that I proudly show to old friends. He notes there is no poster for the Dead concert. I explain that the only reason I have any posters at all is because Julie would always try to remember to take one home from each event I put on. Not so fortunate for the Dead poster, though. Bob tells me he has a great idea: let him recreate one. I think I remember what it looked like, as a lot of Bob's early posters had similar themes and designs. To this day, he has a style that is distinctly his own. After reviewing all the posters, we came up with one to use. Not hard to figure out which one. Anyway, it did not take Bob long to come back with the finished product. What a difference in the computer age

of design. We came to an agreement and partnership and produced a run of this poster. We are still selling this one.

An interesting side note is that the Vancouver Museum has a tribute to the 1960s in the city and as part of the exhibit there is a corner where they recognize the Afterthought and its contribution to the time. The display includes a continuous loop of a film recreation of one of the many hippie houses, featuring a group of hippies talking around the kitchen table. On a wall in the background is the Afterthought Dead poster! Watching this, I realized there was one small problem, namely that I did not produce posters of that size at the time. Nevertheless, it is a very cool looking work, and you can't blame me for trying to recreate history. I am still on a hunt for the original.

While doing research on these posters I went to talk to another old friend, Ron Ulmer. Ron had done light shows for me and we have kept in touch for many years. He related a couple of stories about this time. The first is about the Grateful Dead performance. He attended the dance wearing his new cowboy hat. While Ron was at the show, Pigpen, the Dead's keyboard player, was onstage and trying to get Ron's attention because he saw the hat and liked it. Pigpen asked Ron if they could trade hats. At some time during the

Poster 18b (recreated) ➤

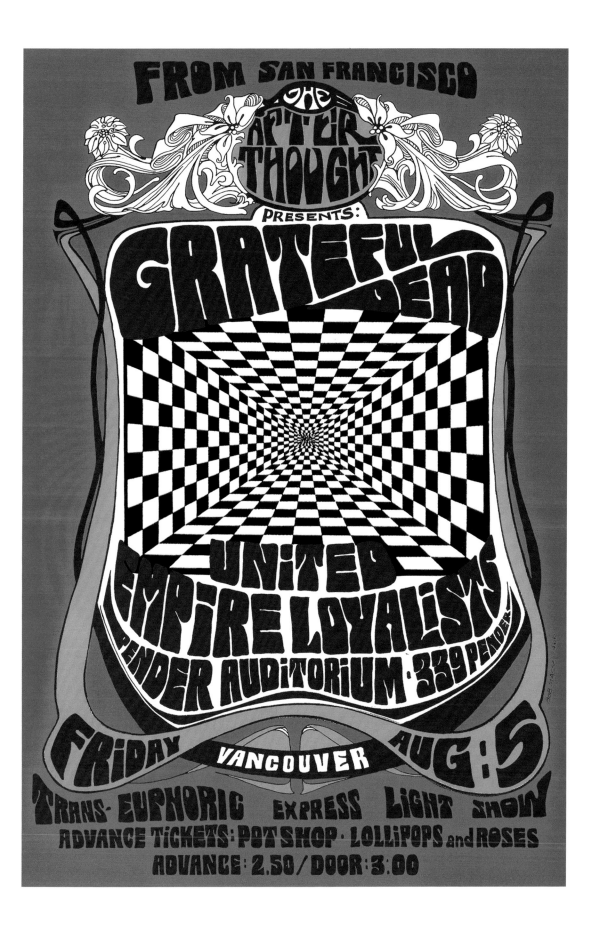

performance they traded their hats old for new. Unfortunately for Ron, he misplaced Pigpen's hat over the years.

Ron also reminisced about the early days of liquid projection. It started out that they would use saran wrap between the liquids they moved around in pie plates over the light projector. Ron observed this and thought why not use the glass faces from large clocks. He tried this and it became the standard for liquid projection. Maybe another Canadian first.

AUGUST 12, 1966: PENDER AUDITORIUM

THE DIMENSIONS FROM SEATTLE

This event was a week after the Dead concert and I was still riding high from the success of that. At the time, no one knew the Dead would go on to become one of the top bands in the world. I still consider the week I spent with them a very special time. I only wish I could remember more of it!

Well now, on to the Dimensions, one of four groups I believe I'd booked when I had driven down to Seattle to meet Pat O'Day, a popular DJ on KJR, the rock and roll station that was happening in the US Pacific Northwest at the time. (See the article by Peter Blecha cited under Related Reading.) O'Day also ran a rock booking outfit much like Les Vogt's Jaguar Agency in Vancouver. (I learned much later that

Poster 19 ▲

Les had a partner that was also a DJ: Red Robinson. Again under Related Reading, see "About Red.") Anyway, O'Day tells me about these great groups he represents, and I book them all and set up the dates. The first one was The Dimensions, a great band and I thought at the time my first group from the States. I don't know why I was thinking that, though, because of course the Dead were my first band from the US, and really they were a much better group to take that honour of being my first import. In early 1966 I felt there were only a few groups that could fill the bill for what I considered the greatest psychedelic dance hall around. What an ego! Still, the Dimensions were a great band for their time.

This poster is again a smaller size from the previous ones, and I was hoping we could continue to use this size. The dance itself was again a great success.

AUGUST 26, 1966: PENDER AUDITORIUM

THE WAILERS AND TOM NORTHCOTT TRIO

This poster is very different from all the other ones because I took pieces of previous posters and pasted them together. I am not sure what I was thinking. I do know I was strung out on speed and I justified this poster because I had a lot going on at the time.

As well as setting up the Afterthought I was looking after the bands for the Teenage Fair at the PNE. I was feeling very important about that gig, and as mentioned earlier it would take me several years to find out I was really only a figurehead for Harry Ornest. He was a very smart man who had the insight to make it look like a teenager like me was running the show, when in fact it was Harry.

Part of my PNE job was to entertain the out-of-town groups, and stories of their goings-on are too numerous to tell. One that stands out, though, was taking one of the early teen heartthrobs of the day out to the Cave nightclub in downtown Vancouver. I am only 18 in a club where they will not serve liquor to anyone under 21. I am wearing one of my tailored silk suits and am sure that to anyone else I look like I am 21. I feel very comfortable sitting at the table with the VIPs and am

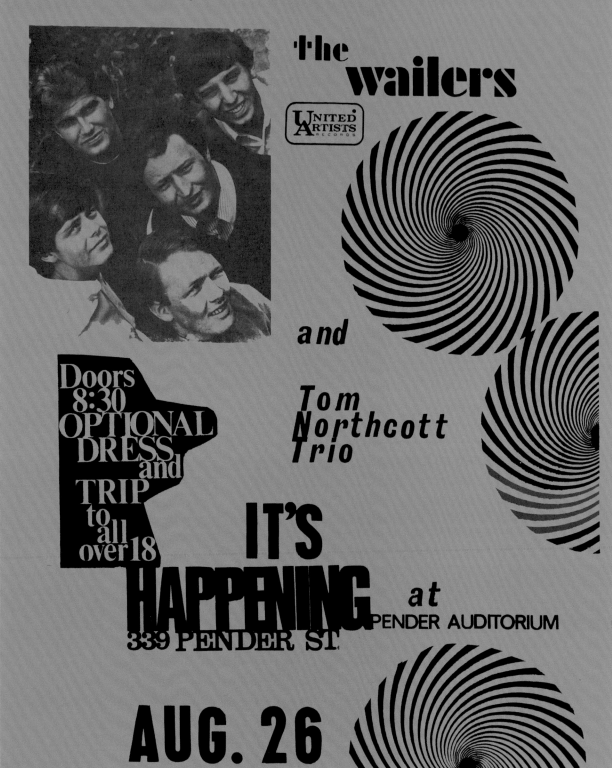

enjoying the proceedings. As the evening progresses I feel the teen heartthrob place his hand on my knee. I push it away and try and figure out what he was doing that for. It was not until much later that I found out he was coming on to me. I was so confused. What a time.

This dance featured the Wailers from Tacoma, my first legitimate recording group, who were signed to United Artists. They did not get the recognition they deserved. I hope they forgave and forgot the way they were treated, for they were a good band, and in spite of the poster and my lack of enthusiasm it was great dance. I seemed to be on a roll bringing in US bands. I am pretty sure that the week before this I had had the Sonics, with a similar poster. I was attempting to do a show every week

◄ *Poster 20*

because of the demand. It seemed I could do no wrong.

Around this time I learned that Sam Perry, who had started my light shows, was not happy with me, because I was adding other people to the light show without his input. Not until I was doing research for this book did I find out he had committed himself to the Crease Clinic for treatment of depression. Like all of us at the time, he had been taking a lot of LSD. When he came to talk to me he was out on a day pass. I often wonder if things would have been different if I had had that information at the time. It turns out that after his argument with me he went home, put a gun to his temple and blew his brains out. I have also just learned that he was 27 at the time. Sam would sadly be the first of many great artists that would take their life at the age of 27.

SEPTEMBER 2, 1966: PENDER AUDITORIUM

THE LIVERPOOL FIVE AND TOM NORTHCOTT TRIO

September, the time when my peers are starting at UBC or a community college. My love is going to UBC to become a teacher. It is not what she wants but it's what her parents want. Coming from a family in which

her mother stayed home and she never had to work, Julie was somewhat spoiled and did what her parents asked of her.

When I was a child, my mother, despite how insane things were, worked very hard to try for us to have a normal family life. She was a strong, liberated single mom at a time when this was far from the norm. She had to deal with an abusive estranged husband and with my brother, who just wanted to stay stoned all the time rather than confront his own issues from childhood. When the dance hall was booming in the spring of 1966 all my close friends were graduating from high school. This would not happen for me until much later in life, when I graduated from night school. By that time I would be a husband and father trying to get ahead in life. This was a very hard time for me and the road ahead was about to get a whole lot crazier.

The Liverpool Five were a group from England touring the Northwest. I was able to get them when I was in Seattle booking bands. Given the time, and the popularity of anything British, I do believe it would have helped the show if I had pointed out that the group were in fact from England. Instead I give them equal billing with the Tom Northcott Trio. It seems I was more interested in the poster design than in who I offered top billing to.

I know I was attempting to deal with the death of Sam Perry, the first of many close friends I would lose to drug abuse. For the record, staying stoned was not then and is still not now the way to fix a problem. In the case of most of the good friends I lost, their deaths could have been prevented had they been able to deal with their demons. Instead they found it easier to just stay stoned.

Back to the poster, my intent was to have it look like a liquid projection as a tribute to Sam. I could not bring myself to tell anybody that I cared about anything. I was starting to become very callous, building a very hard shell around myself and thinking that my hand-tailored silk suits would protect me. I am not sure why. And of course I had the drugs to help me cope with whatever I needed to cope with. In spite of everything, the dance was another great success. I believe it was Bruce Dowad who did this poster for me. I recall spending a lot of time telling the designer how I wanted it to look.

Poster 21 ➤

SEPTEMBER 16 1966: PENDER AUDITORIUM

BLACK SNAKE BLUES BAND AND UNITED EMPIRE LOYALISTS

I had completed my first contract job looking after the bands at the PNE's Teenage Fair and it was an incredible experience. I walked away with a lot of money and a very swelled head, not that it needed to get any bigger. Harry told me he would see me next year and was looking forward to working with me again. He also told me to keep an eye on Tommy Chong, as he thought he had great potential, and asked me to make sure Tommy's group, Bobby Taylor and the Vancouvers, would be available for next year. Harry also suggested I should use them in my dance hall, but I never booked them, because I thought they were too rhythm and blues, too straight.

I had used groups from Vancouver's Jaguar Enterprises and from the US Northwest, but the act that was by far the biggest hit to date was the Dead. Everybody in town was still talking about what a great show it was. I needed to find more blues bands, which at the time were the only type of attraction that was fitting the psychedelic bill. The only true psychedelic band locally was the United Empire Loyalists, which happened to be the group I managed. My peers and the older patrons

in their 20s wanted more blues bands, not the straight bands that dominated Vancouver at the time! It was at about this time that I was approached by a brand new outfit that claimed they could do blues. Joe Conroy was on guitar and was also the vocalist. I didn't believe they had any experience, but then neither did the Loyalists until I booked them. So I said yes to Conroy and now I have a show I can put on: this new group called the Black Snake Blues Band and the United Empire Loyalists. I decided I would let Black Snake open.

It was also during this time that I came up with the idea of selling memberships for the Afterthought. Patrons could purchase a card that would get them into the dances at a reduced rate. For this event I was convinced I should only charge $1 for members, which hopefully would induce more people to buy memberships. Their membership would also entitle them to free pop. It was easy to do a giveaway like this, as Coca Cola had introduced me to their newest thing for concession stands: the pop dispenser with H_2O. I was now

Poster 22 ➤

the
BLACK SNAKE BLUES BAND
& the
# UNITED EMPIRE LOYALISTS

with the Mystic Trip Out Reunion

The AFTERTHOUGHT
339 W PENDER
ADMISSION ONLY
$1.00 with membership
SEPT. 16
DOORS OPEN 8:30

selling pop by the glass and every glass was costing me only pennies.

So now I have a new lineup, and the venue and date are locked in. All I need is a poster. Again I have Bruce Dowad, the bass player for the Loyalists, create one. At the time, it felt like everyone wanted to be an artist. I believe that at the time Bruce was only 16, but why not? I was all of 18 myself.

The dance was a big hit and another blues band was born!

The word is now out there that the Afterthought is the place to be. Everyone wants a dance every week, but I have a problem: I cannot get the Pender every weekend. What to do? Find another hall. I had found them before so why not again?

On Fourth Ave a new store had just opened called the Psychedelic Shop. It was owned by Doug Hawthorne, one of the first people in town with shoulder-length

hair. I believe he had just arrived from Edmonton and had opened up a sandal shop called the Blind Owl. He would later end up working on my light shows and became a good friend. Unfortunately, he too would become another victim of the times.

The Psychedelic Shop was rapidly becoming the in spot for a rapidly growing hippie community. Across the street there was a community hall owned by the local Russian immigrant community. They were having problems renting out the place because of a backlash of local paranoia about communism, so they were more than willing to rent to me on a regular basis. The fact that my heritage is Ukrainian also helped. See page 60 for the story of how this new venue began.

Psychedelic Shop opening ▼

SEPTEMBER 23, 1966: PENDER AUDITORIUM

THE JABBERWOCK AND BLACK SNAKE BLUES BAND

This will be my last dance at the Pender. I have put on at least 15 shows at this venue and a lot has changed in my life. The Boilermakers Union were always very supportive and wished me well, but they could not provide the hall for all the dates I needed it for that the Afterthought members wanted, which was at least a dance every week plus more. Yes, I said "members," for somewhere along the line at the Pender, as mentioned earlier, I had come up with the idea of selling memberships to belong to the Afterthought. I am not certain now, but I believe I charged $5 for the card and members would then get a reduced rate to get into the dance. I was very proud of this because it was giving me cash upfront to better prepare for the dances, and it gave me some operating capital.

Dealing with the cash was very difficult for me because I had no concept about saving for a rainy day. I had always had trouble saving and still do to this day. I never was able to learn this very important skill, for at that time I was more interested in spending money as fast as it came in. I was developing a taste for a lot of different drugs and had no idea of what they were

doing to me. One I really liked was what was then called "speed." It made it possible for me to get things done a lot faster, or so I thought. It also created a lot of paranoia, which I had no idea was a side effect. My solution for dealing with this was to drop more acid – in retrospect not a good idea, but of course nobody could tell an 18-year-old anything (especially me!), because I really believed I knew everything. I still had so much to learn.

For my last event at the Pender the Black Snake Blues Band were a huge hit, so after the show everybody told me they wanted to hear more of them. Rock and blues were in demand along with psychedelia. So I hired Jabberwock and set up the Black Snakes as the headliner, even though it was only their second gig. Things really did happen quickly, or so I believed at the time.

With the bands booked, I go with Bruce Dowad again for the poster, for he works cheap and I figure the last poster was okay so why not again. Bob Masse, meanwhile, is working very hard to convince me that he was indeed going to be the best poster designer. Who knew how big he would become?! I agreed he could do the next poster, for the grand opening of the Afterthought at the Kits Theatre.

As this was my last dance at the Pender, I only charged $1 for members. What a deal! Again the event was a great success and I really believed I could do no wrong.

It would not be until many years later that dances such as mine would return to the Pender Auditorium. Alas, they were not my dances, though they would nevertheless use the Afterthought name.

Poster 23 ➤

SEPTEMBER 23, 1966: THE LIGHTHOUSE

PAINTED SHIP

The Lighthouse was the name of a psychedelic coffeehouse and hippie light show across the street from the Afterthought on Fourth Avenue. I am not sure to this day what it really was. It was owned and operated by Doug Hawthorne. There were all kinds of rumours as to where Doug was from and about his past. I guess I could have just asked him, but the rumours were more fun. Some of the stories were that he was a former Hells Angel from Edmonton who wanted to join the hippie movement, and that he did this by opening a few business operations on Fourth Avenue, one in the next block, one down the street and one right across the street. The only one I cared about was the Lighthouse, as I saw it as direct competition to my dance hall. So

I went over and introduced myself and told him of my concerns. He had a simple solution: give him a job by hiring his light show and he would stay closed on the nights I was open. Also that I had to book the band he was managing, Painted Ship. Seemed like a straightforward proposition. We shook hands and the Trans Euphoric Express light show was now playing at the Afterthought.

Rumours about Doug Hawthorne continue to this day. When I tried to find him to interview him for this book and renew my friendship, as he was a good guy, I was told he had perished in a small-plane crash in South America. Another story had it that the crash had been in northern California. Who knows what the truth is. But he did have a child while in Vancouver,

so perhaps that person will be able to set the record straight some day.

These changes are all things that occurred back then and played out like scenes from a movie. Come to think of it, those were such crazy times that maybe they *were* a movie. I had even heard rumours in later years that I too was dead, when all I'd done was left Vancouver.

Poster 24 ➤

SEPTEMBER 30, 1966: KITS THEATRE

UNITED EMPIRE LOYALISTS AND THE NOCTURNALS

The owners of our brand new venue, the Russian Canadian club, appeared to be much more open to letting me make changes to their hall. I begin these by shining a strobe light, in what I believe was a first in Canada, onto a mirrored ball like the ones made famous in the dance halls of the 1920s. I had to have both ball and light custom made, as you could not just walk into a store and buy these things. You could purchase a black light, however, so we got one of those too. The light show gear was now situated on the balcony, which meant it could project onto three of the four walls of the venue.

I needed to improve the sound system, though, which was really lacking. I knew I could not duplicate the Dead's audio, but I hoped to come close. I chose to go to Kelly Deyong, which had the best sound equipment in the city at that time. This company would go on to supply audio for all the major acts coming into BC. I obtained two large speaker boxes, four feet by six feet with radial horns on top, the biggest PA system I could find at the time. [For more on Paul Deyong and Vancouver sound gear, see page 209 in the Afterwords section.]

The poster too needed to be great so everyone would find out about the new venue. Up to this time I had tried several formats and designers, including myself, and was looking for someone to take the artwork up a notch. Bob Masse had been telling me for some time that he was the best one for the job. When I informed him I was happy with the guy I had, he told me he could do a better job than anybody else and that he would do the first poster for

free. How could I turn down an offer like that?

Exactly how I met Bob is a little hazy. He had come to a dance and introduced himself. Said he was an up-and-coming graphic designer who was going to art school and had teamed up with another designer, Doug Matheson, working as a company called Masse & Matheson.

As I say, Bob agreed to do the first poster for free to prove how good he was, and if I was happy with the results I would pay him $50 for each camera-ready poster. I would also retain the originals and the rights to all reproduction. We shook hands on the deal.

Years later, when I first talked to Bob about this, he thought the second-last poster he did for me was the first one, or at least that was how it showed on his website, www.bmasse.com. He has since corrected the website and it now does not show a first poster at all. The only thing I know for sure is that I have worked really hard at remembering an awfully eventful past and I find it strange how certain things came to mind instantly, like Bob telling me he would do the first poster for free! I also clearly remember that I told all my poster artists that all of the rights to the posters were mine. When I look back I figure it was a pretty advanced business move for an 18-year-old kid. Who knew that Bob Masse would go on to become one of the leading poster artists ever. And he's Canadian, of course.

I had to open the new venue with the band I was managing, the United Empire Loyalists. I felt obligated to include a band from Les Vogt too, so I booked the Nocturnals on Les's recommendation. The Nocturnals went on to play at Expo 67 in Montreal. They broke up shortly after that, though, because they did not want to play "that psychedelic music" that was going strong in 1967. This seemed odd at the time, as I had had them perform a number of times in my psychedelic dance hall. This band were also part owners of the Grooveyard, which was Les Vogt's straight teen club located in New Westminster.

For this show, I had Bob put on the poster that the first 12 couples would receive free admission and free refreshments. This was harder than you would think, because back then not everyone came as couples.

With all the incentives and advertising it appeared that everyone loved the show. It was a great success and most important to me the hall was full. The move had worked and we were located in the hot new spot on Fourth Avenue in Kitsilano, which was becoming Vancouver's answer to San Francisco's Haight Ashbury.

The big challenge would come a week later with a dance on both Friday and Saturday nights. I knew I was getting into pretty deep water and that I would need help.

Poster 25 ➤

NEW AFTERTHOUGHT HAPPENING

GRAND OPENING !!
FRIDAY SEPT. 30
KITSILANO THEATRE
2114 WEST FOURTH

UNITED EMPIRE LOYALISTS

Liquid projections
STROBE LIGHT
TRIP-OUT
Slides
FREEK OUT
DANCE
LIGHT SHOW
BLACK LIGHT
HAPPENING

NOCTURNALS
★ FIRST 12 COUPLES FREE ★
★ FREE REFRESHMENTS ★
8:30 - 1:00
18 & OVER

BOB MASSE

OCTOBER 7 AND 8, 1966: KITS THEATRE

PAINTED SHIP AND UNITED EMPIRE LOYALISTS; BITTER SWEETS AND WILLIAM TELL & THE MARKSMEN

One week has gone by and here I am doing my 20th show and by tomorrow night I will have completed my 21st. As you can see, top billing was a new light show and a new band in keeping with my agreement with Doug Hawthorne. There were of course some problems with the other people I had had doing the light show. I knew I had to do some very careful negotiations with everyone involved, as I had already lost Sam Perry. I did not want anything unforeseen to happen. These were all good people and I knew I had to make it work for everyone. I am still not sure what exactly I did, but I do not remember having any more trouble with light shows.

All of this was nevertheless very stressful for me, though I did not realize this at the time. I just got stoned a lot to help me cope and would not let anyone tell me anything. My brother was trying to help and he wanted to be a partner. This was something I did not want, because I knew he was into much more serious drugs and no one could tell him anything either, especially me. I had taken on one partner who had had a minor part in the Afterthought, but after the move to Fourth Avenue he had gone on to other things. Still, he was there when I needed him. I thought that as long as I kept control of the company, all would be okay, so I took on another partner, Jon York, who considered himself a professional folksinger and said he would look after the bands. Jon also became a victim of the times, as he would die from an overdose several years later. He was a good guy and I still miss him.

The story goes, or at least what Jon told me, was that he had been working a very boring job in Toronto and was married, just another straight dude that was not happy. He told me he went for a walk one day and just never went home. He took a train or bus, not sure which, and came west. One day in the grocery store he saw a tin of York brand beans, and that's when he decided to change his name from Jepson to York. With someone he had met along the way he then formed the folksinging duo of York & Beans. They were a pretty good act, working the coffee house circuit.

Poster 26 ➤

AFTERTHOUGHT PRESENTS

TRANS
EUPHORIC
EXPRESS

LIGHT DANCE SHOW

FRIDAY OCT. 7th

PAINTEDSHIP

AND THE

UNITED EMPIRE LOYALISTS

SATURDAY OCT. 8

BITTERSWEETS

WILLIAM TELL
AND THE
MARKSMEN

AT THE

Kitsilano theatre

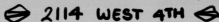

2114 WEST 4TH

I soon found out Jon was quite a bit older than me, but he was a good friend and I learned a lot from him.

We did the two nights in a row that weekend and it was quite the experience. Very overwhelming. But somehow I pulled it off, with two new bands making their debut performances at the Afterthought. The city was starting to develop a new sound of blues and psychedelia. It was starting to happen. Vancouver was growing up and so was I.

OCTOBER 14 AND 15, 1966: KITS THEATRE

CENTAURS AND BLACK SNAKE BLUES BAND

We are getting ready for the third dance at the Kits. First we line up the bands. Headlining will be the Centaurs, the band I booked when I first went on my own. They wanted to play again on this date, as it would be their last Vancouver appearance before they went on a European tour. I thought it was pretty special that a local Canadian group were going to get international exposure. They would be the first of many local bands that would go on to perform all over the world. Second on the bill would be the Black Snake Blues Band, the newest act we'd been hiring, who continued to be a great hit.

Bob Masse had now done all of the posters for the new venue and they were getting great reviews. Bob would become the resident poster artist for the Afterthought.

I said "we" back in that first paragraph because I had now taken on a third partner, Roger Schiffer, another friend of my brother's and the most interesting of all my Afterthought associates. Roger told me I needed him because he had an accounting background and experience looking after money. I never questioned whether this was true or not. It seems I never really questioned anybody or checked out how truthful they were. As I look back I have mostly always taken people at face value and believed what they told me was the truth. Something I was told about Roger much later on – and I have never been able to verify this – was that he was really using the dancehall as a location to deal dope. I was still very naive. And I had trouble

Poster 27 ➤

with Roger pretty much from the start of this partnership. Previously I had just done whatever I thought was best for the dancehall, but now, for the first time, I had someone questioning the choices I was making. This was indeed very difficult for an 18-year-old kid who essentially thought he knew everything. Why wouldn't I think that? After all, the vast majority of the events were a success. They ran well, everybody seemed like they were having a good time, and of course I was making a profit. So what could be wrong?

When I reflect back as to why I was taking on partners in the first place, it was really just to keep my brother, Terry, out of the business. Just my way of not helping with his addictions, for it was far too hard to accept the problems he was having. I would end up with the same addictions even though I said it could never happen to me. And I was soon about to learn a very hard lesson about what problems partners could become. The one thing I did do to protect myself was to form a limited company and retain the majority share.

Roger nevertheless brought two good ideas to the table. One was to have a button that said "Light, Show, Dance," with the first letter of each word capitalized and highlighted: LSD. How cool is that, I thought, and indeed it was a great marketing tool. However, this too would come back to get me into a lot of trouble with the establishment. I was still having to deal with the fallout from my very first Tom Northcott poster, the one with the flowers coming out of Tom's head. Of course I must be suggesting people should get stoned. Roger's other good idea was to use postcard-size posters. Naturally, I did not agree at the time, but I learned I could also be wrong. Roger Schiffer passed away in 1994 after a long battle with cancer.

One smart thing I did when I moved the dancehall to the Kits was to put my mother in the ticket booth in charge of the cash. She was the best person to take care of this, for if you can't trust your mother, who can you trust? My mother passed away in 2002 and would be very proud of this accounting of my life. But I see her being proudest of Julie's and my family, which in a very strange way evolved from the Afterthought.

OCTOBER 21, 1966: KITS THEATRE

TOM NORTHCOTT TRIO AND PAINTED SHIP

We were ready to do it again, this time for only the Friday with two bands instead of the two nights we had been doing. Not sure why the change; there were some small disagreements but everyone appeared to be fine with how the dances were running. We had to repeat bands more often than I would have liked, but there were only so many acts that fit the bill. There were more new ones on the horizon, however. Northcott had been around from the start, of course, but he was very good at making his music evolve and not get stagnant. Painted Ship were the new kids on the block but were developing their own following. [See Anders F., "Interview with William Hay (Painted Ship)" in Related Reading.]

The Afterthought posters had continued to improve since Bob Masse started doing them. You could now see the start of what would become known as psychedelic art. This is the first poster where Bob introduced visuals (note the angels with sunglasses). This was the start of many great posters that continue to sell today. I never thought that what we were producing for advertising dances would be saved and thought of as an art form and become collectible.

The city was changing, with lots of new nightlife. Tommy Chong invited me to his after-hours club called the Elegant Parlour. This became a regular spot I went to after I'd finished for the night at the Afterthought.

I was still not old enough to attend clubs, as the legal age was 21. Tommy's brother would tell me to just sit in the back and watch the bands jam. I was fortunate to listen to some fantastic sessions. I would learn later that I would often be followed by Abe Snidanko, of the Vancouver police drug squad, who would later be immortalized in the Cheech & Chong movies as the caricature head of the drug squad. At the time, he would indeed be a very dangerous person to what was considered the counterculture. All Abe could think of was that he had to stamp us out – in other words, bust everybody he could. He would later tell me it had been his personal mission to get my dance hall closed down at any cost, for he was convinced it was corrupting the youth of Vancouver.

What was even stranger was that Vancouver policeman Don Bellamy was always very supportive of the dance hall. He felt it was a good thing because he always knew where the kids were. Don went on to become an alderman and president of the Vancouver Restaurant Association. I continued to keep in touch with him and was privileged to have him come to the Comox Valley to speak in support of an alternative sentencing program for youth. Don was and is a very good person.

◄ *Poster 28*

OCTOBER 28, 1966: KITS THEATRE

UNITED EMPIRE LOYALISTS AND THE BLUE KNIGHTS BAND

Now that I had a team to work with, we began to plan several events in advance, coming up with promotion ideas etc. In other words, running like a regular business. I had trouble with this because I had no experience working with a team and I liked having my own way. In looking back, I am sure it was difficult for everyone, because what we were doing was a first for all of us. All we could do was our best.

We lined up the bookings. There was a new outfit called the Blue Knights Band, which I have no memory of or information on, and of course the United Empire Loyalists. Bob as usual did a great poster with what I felt was a folk motif. I thought I recognized my partner Jon York in it.

This whole event was more of a blur than usual, as I was about to get busted.

As best we can tell, Jon and I had left the dance hall after what had become our regular weekly meeting. I'm not sure why, but he invited me to his house for coffee and I decided to ride with him because he had a vintage Bentley in perfect condition. We made quite the scene riding through town in that car, as I was a short, skinny kid and Jon was 6 foot 6. Anyway, off we go to his apartment in the west end. As we start to drive Jon says he thinks we are being followed, just like a scene from one of the movies Tommy Chong would make some years later. We drove around for a while, and once we were confident we had lost them, we proceeded to Jon's place. As a status symbol I always carried a small amount of pot in a baggie, enough for a couple of joints. When I wore my three-piece tailored suits it was routine that I kept it in my vest pocket. I was confident that if I were ever followed I would have time to flush it, which was also the normal thing to do given the time. Jon parks the car and we walk up to his place. We are greeted by his lady and we enter the apartment. Before we can close the door Abe Snidanko is in my face and pulling the bag of pot out of my pocket. Next thing I know, I am handcuffed and being told I am under arrest. They next searched the apartment and found more pot, so Jon too is arrested. We are taken into custody and driven to the main police station. I was completely terrified and it felt like my worst nightmare.

When we arrived at the station I was only focused on what was happening to me, so I lost track of Jon. I remember being asked to step to the side by two cops. They told me to take off my jacket, which they searched. Then they proceeded to tell me to take off clothing piece by piece until I stood there naked. They then looked into every opening of my body. I was terrified; I could not believe what was happening. It appeared to me that the two cops were very much enjoying this. I started shaking and I was given back my socks, underwear, pants and shirt. I was then locked up in what I later learned was a holding cell. In the cell I was befriended by two other kids. One of them had somehow gotten some matches and proceeded to

start a fire. Within minutes the cops came and asked who started the fire. Of course no one would say a word, so the cops of course concluded it must have been one of us three kids. We were all taken out of the cell and told each of us would be segregated until one of us would admit he did it. I was placed in what I believe was an empty broom closet and told I would remain there until someone said who started the fire! I ended up spending the night in that closet. It was apparent that whoever had been in the closet before me had peed on the floor, so I could not even sit down. This was a very traumatic time for me and I had no idea that this event would haunt me for the rest of life. Until now the only people I have only ever told this story to are my soulmate, Julie, and a psychologist who in 1986 was treating me for post-traumatic stress from when I was taken hostage while working as a senior corrections officer. That is a whole other story. It was that psychologist who, after he heard my life story, concluded I had suffered from PTS many times in my youth and the hostage incident had been just the icing on the cake.

The next morning, I was released on bail. My mother had put her house up for collateral for the amount. I was picked up by my father and he drove me to my mother's house. I was a wreck.

Poster 29 ➤

Just an afterthought as I write this story: it has been 46 years almost to the day since this happened. What is most interesting is that this very week in the US, two states made it legal to possess up to one ounce of cannabis for personal use. Yes, the times they are changing, and sometimes it takes a long, long time. [See, for example, the CBC News article by Daniel Schwartz cited in Related Reading.]

NOVEMBER 4, 1966: KITS THEATRE

WILLIAM TELL & THE MARKSMEN AND GREAT WHITE LIGHT

Here we go again, another great poster. Bob is really starting to show his creativity. The first of two somewhat new bands is William Tell & The Marksmen, some of the members of which would go on to bands like the Seeds of Time, Papa Bear's Medicine Show and Prism. The other new band for this show, Great White Light, I have no memory of, in spite of my research. This should not be surprising, as I had just been busted and charged with possession of cannabis (under half an ounce). After spending the night in jail and being released on bail, with my mother having to pledge her house for the money, I was not in the best of shape. It was a wonder I was coping at all. What I found to be totally ironic was that all I wanted to do was get more stoned on what I had been busted for and find something stronger, perhaps what my brother had discovered as his means of coping with what he considered to be a crazy world.

Terry was 15 or 16 when he was busted the first time. I remember visiting him at juvenile hall and him telling me I had no idea what it was all about. Now I did have some idea. I also understood why he would continue to get arrested on into adulthood, and understood the reason why he would continue to go to jail again and again. Yes, he was committing what was considered petty theft in order to support his drug habit. At least I could justify my bust as political because I was fighting the system for what I believed in. I had a right to smoke pot and it was nobody else's concern. As I said, it seems strange 46 years later that two US states now agree with me and I am finally not

Poster 30 ➤

afraid to write about this horrific part of my past.

The stress of these events could also explain why I have such a hard time today remembering CBC television coming to my dance hall. They had travelled all the way from Toronto to do a documentary on my business. The only memory I have is standing in front of the camera in the dance hall being interviewed and being told what a wonderful thing I was doing. I would learn much later what a price I would have to pay for what I was told was so wonderful!

NOVEMBER 9, 1966: PIPEDREAM PRESENTS AT THE QUEEN ELIZABETH THEATRE

JEFFERSON AIRPLANE, MUDDY WATERS AND TOM NORTHCOTT TRIO

The hippie movement was defiantly getting more organized. Pipedream, comprised of a group of friends who worked at the Afterthought, had taken another step into promotion. This was very hard for me to swallow, as I was still under the very stupid illusion that I was the only one who could control the psychedelic movement. But as you can see from this beautiful poster, incredible talent lineup and great venue, Pipedream had indeed come a long way from the Trips Festival. Some members of this group would morph into Intermedia, a co-operative that raised the level of the arts in Vancouver for a number of years. [See, for example, the *Ruins in Process* and Gregg Simpson entries in

Related Reading.] The concert did appear to be quite a success compared to the Trips Festival, and both the Jefferson Airplane and Muddy Waters would indeed go on to become legends. The timing of the show, on a Wednesday, did not affect attendance at our dance the next night, possibly because it was in a classy sit-down venue and thus drew an older crowd in their late twenties.

Recalling this event caused me to jump ahead ten years to approximately 1976. At that time I had a job as a financial aid worker for the provincial government in Courtenay, BC. My function was

Poster 31 ➤

the pipe-dream presents

8:30 pm

$$ 52., 2·50, 3., 3·50, 4.

Jefferson Airplane

Muddy Waters

Tom Northcott Trio

queen elizabeth theatre

NOVEMBER 9, 1966.

Tickets   the Vancouver Ticket Centre: 630 Hamilton & all Eaton's Stores   VIS

to approve client eligibility for financial assistance for whoever applied. One my first clients I remember very well was in his late twenties and living on Denman Island. When I asked why he was applying for social assistance he told me he had had trouble keeping it together ever since he became a regular at this dance hall in Vancouver called the Afterthought. "Very interesting," I said, without cracking up, and immediately approved his application. He must have gotten it together, though, because he only remained on my caseload a short time.

How things do change, for by that time my promotion days were behind me. I was happily married, with two children and another on the way. As I write this I am still happily married and have eight grandchildren. Yes indeed, things do take time.

NOVEMBER 10, 11, 13, 1966: KITS THEATRE

BLACK SNAKE BLUES BAND, PAINTED SHIP, UNITED EMPIRE LOYALISTS, HUMAN MIND

I have no idea why I decided to go for Thursday, Friday and Sunday on this weekend. Could it have been because was the Remembrance Day long weekend and the venue was rented to someone else on the Saturday, as the poster clearly states "No Dance on Saturday"? I am not even sure if Human Mind was a band or if I was trying to make some statement.

This was a great poster but unfortunately it was one Julie did not save. We did find it for sale online, however, by someone in London, England, for what I thought was a large sum of money. I have always wondered how my posters seem to have made it to so many parts of the world.

We are all prepared to do a big show for both days. We seemed to have everything in place. The first night goes off without any problems. However, the second night was about to become a large problem. The dance hall filled up as expected and everyone was having a good time. I remember going outside as I usually would do to see if there were more customers coming. Up at the intersection to my left I could see the police had blocked off the street from

Poster 32 ➤

traffic. I then looked to my right and again the traffic was stopped. I turned to go back into the dance hall and right beside me is Abe Snidanko and his sidekick, Constable Brown, who are telling me they will escort me back inside. What I was not aware of was that my mother, all four and a half feet of her, was watching all this from the ticket booth. As I was escorted back into the dance hall we were followed by the Vancouver police. They put me up against the wall, telling me not to move. Terry appeared out of nowhere and they put him up against the wall beside me. They then went into the dance hall and ordered everyone to stand up against the wall. Snidanko and Brown proceeded to search me and my brother. At that, my mother came storming out from the ticket booth and asked Abe what he was doing. He informed her that they were looking for drugs. It was then that my mother started to speak to Abe in Ukrainian. She did not hold back in her native tongue. She somehow knew that Snidanko also was Ukrainian, and to my surprise he clearly could understand everything she was saying. She told him he should be ashamed of himself, as her boys were not doing anything wrong and that there were no drugs here. I was just grateful that I got to keep my clothes on

this time! Fortunately neither I nor Terry was carrying any drugs. I had learned my lesson from last time. Of course, that first bust did not stop my drug intake – in fact it just increased it – but it did make me more careful. The good news was that this big takedown, again like something right out of the movies, yielded no drugs. After much reflection over many years I thought about what this must have cost the taxpayers. What a waste of resources. The only conclusion I could come to as to why the police picked that weekend was the extra overtime they would all be getting paid because of the holiday weekend. This incident, I would soon learn, was only the beginning of police harassment in what they considered to be a "war on drugs."

Just an afterthought: in the sixties cannabis was an import product not an export product. Nowadays everyone knows "BC bud" as one of the province's great exports. I can only conclude, given the present-day climate, that the police are no closer to winning their war on drugs now than they were back then. [See the Janelle Jordan CBC News article in Related Reading.]

What with everything that was going on that weekend, it was no wonder Julie did not save a copy of the poster.

NOVEMBER 25, 1966: KITS THEATRE

TOM NORTHCOTT TRIO AND BRAVE NEW WORLD

Here we finally get going again, this time after quite a long interval between shows. That's what happens when your dance hall gets busted only a short time after you'd got busted yourself. Things like this can make one very paranoid. I was pretty sure the dance hall regulars would be a little nervous too, to say the least.

During this time off I had gone for another road trip to Seattle. Next to San Francisco, Seattle was the happening place. They had a lot more of what I considered hip bands. One of these was Brave New World, and I do believe I was the first to bring them to Canada. Seattle was getting a good reputation for their bands, for let us not forget that Jimi Hendrix got his start there. And yes, he did come up to Vancouver around this time. I never booked him, but of course I wish I had. I do remember Julie coming back from a church youth group conference she attended in Seattle and telling me about hearing this great guitarist playing in a church basement. I guess I should have paid more attention to Julie and what she was telling me. She always did know best; it would just take me a long time to learn this.

Once I'd booked my group, I was off to the Seattle university campus for some of the best LSD and pot in the Northwest. Yes, universities on the west coast were much more than bastions of higher learning. Unless you interpret getting high as higher learning. For any young people reading this, it is *not* an endorsement for getting stoned. I'm just telling you that getting stoned does not fix your problems. It took me a long time to learn this, and I hope this book will help others learn it also.

I return to Vancouver to put on the next Afterthought show. In spite of Brave New World, this dance was not a success. It was also the start of getting rid of my final partner, Roger Schiffer. I was convinced that the face on this poster looked like him. Only many years later would I find out that the picture was in fact a profile of Charlie Chaplin's daughter Geraldine. I now know I should have asked him at the time, as it would have made things much easier. Did I not tell you at the beginning of this story that paranoia can play many tricks on your mind? Maybe that's why that Steve Stills/Buffalo Springfield song "For What It's Worth" was such a hit.

NO AFTERTHOUGHT DANCE ON SATURDAY
AFTERTHOUGHT
FRIDAY - NOV. 25
8:30 PM
TOM NORTHCOTT TRIO
BRAVE NEW WORLD
LIGHT SHOW
TRANS - EUPHORIC EXPRESS
KITSILANO THEATRE 2114 W. 4th
POSTER DESIGNED BY BOB MASSE
NO AFTERTHOUGHT DANCE ON SATURDAY

My first partner, Dennis Vance, just seemed to move on to other adventures.

◄ *Poster 33*

Jon York would end up in jail after pleading guilty to possession after our bust together. I do believe he thought it would help me. Problems with Roger still lay ahead.

DECEMBER 2, 1966: KITS THEATRE

UNITED EMPIRE LOYALISTS AND UNFORESEEN

Bob Masse is definitely coming of age with his posters. He has now created what I believe to be his first three-colour one. He accomplished this by using a colour paper stock and then using blue and black ink to get the effect of three colours. The beautiful lady on the poster is Julie Christie, something I learned from Bob only about 10 years ago.

I am still feeling the effects of the two busts. I know Abe Snidanko is on a mission to close the dance hall down, and that one way to do this is to have me convicted of possession of cannabis. If he succeeds, the city will revoke the Afterthought's licence, which is in my name. This of course is creating friction between me and Roger, who wants control of the hall, as he feels I will be convicted. Then I realize he was not at the hall when it was busted. Roger was also one of a few people who knew I had always carried a small amount of pot

in my vest pocket. Could he have known in advance about the bust? As I said before, these were times of paranoia and it is indeed difficult to know what was real and what was not. Roger tells me I have two choices: either he gets control of the company or I can buy him out for $1,000. In 1966 this was a lot of money, and I did not have it. Unfortunately I had not saved any when I had the opportunity to do so. But I had worked for over a year to build this dance hall business and now Roger, a minor partner for only four months who had put in no money, wants control or $1,000.

My lawyer, Gary Lauk, a family friend, does not know if I can beat the possession charge but knows he can delay the trial until the spring. I decide to buy Roger out, for I had worked too hard to lose control. My mother loaned me the funds. She was not happy with what had happened but nevertheless was always supportive. Today,

as father and grandfather, I have a very deep understanding of what she had to endure with her two sons. She was an amazing mother and I still miss her very much.

◀ *Poster 34*

I am blessed that she was also a fantastic grandmother, with much insight which she shared with our grandchildren.

So now the Afterthought is again mine alone, and I have learned a hard lesson. There will be no more partners for me.

DECEMBER 1966

THE BARNETT BROTHERS
MERRILEE & THE TURNABOUTS

Everything at the Afterthought was starting to improve, No more partners, better shows on the horizon. I just had the possession charges to deal with in the future. So when the Barnett brothers showed up at a dance I was a little taken by surprise.

I knew both Jeffery and Peter as the owners of Pizza Patio, a little takeout shop where you could buy small, single-serving pizzas. I remember talking with Jeffery many years later, wanting to give them credit for starting the single-size, six-inch pizza concept. Jeffrey very modestly said they did not originate the idea, but I believe they were the ones that made it mainstream.

These twin brothers would go on to be successful restaurant entrepreneurs and do great benefit work in local communities as well. Back in the day, however, they were just two dedicated guys with

a dream of making pizza. But when they came to me saying they wanted to buy Afterthought Enterprises Inc. and have me work for them, my answer was a quick "No, thank you," given everything that had just happened to me with partners. They persisted, though, and became my competition. But more importantly, many years later they would become good friends, and friendship like theirs you cannot buy.

Peter and Jeffery had decided they too would try the rock and roll promotion scene and booked Merrilee & The Turnabouts into the Garden Auditorium at the PNE grounds. This show was not a success.

The Turnabouts were a hard-working Seattle band fronted by Merrilee Rush on keyboards and vocals. Rush would have an international top-ten hit in 1968 with "Angel of the Morning" and was Grammy

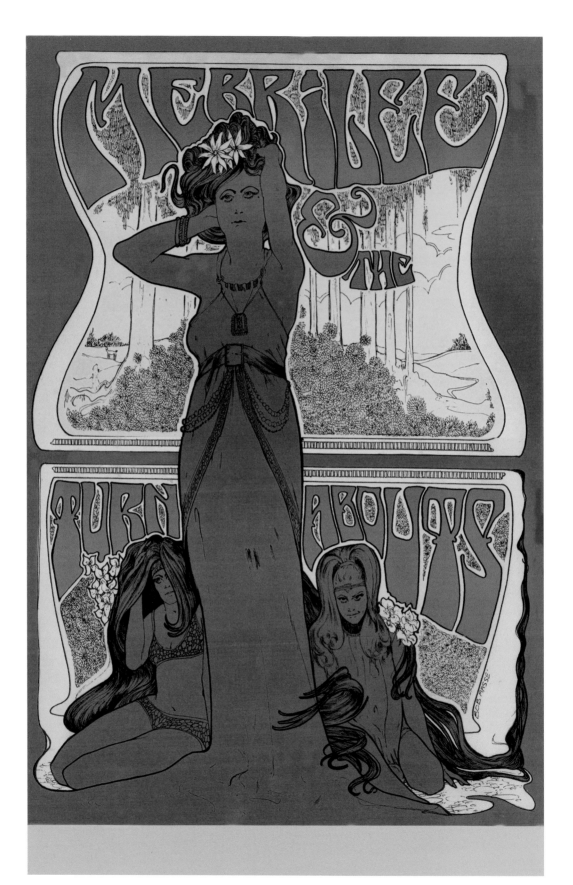

nominated for female vocalist of the year. She continues to perform and record today. Centaurs organist Bob Brown has posted a nice tribute to Merrilee at a great music website you should visit called Pacific Northwest Bands, pnwbands.com:

> I saw and talked to Merrilee Rush at the Hollywood Bowl/Grooveyard in about 1965 or '66. She was gracious and professional and had her small child at the gig with her. Her husband was in the band. He was very protective of her and it was sweet to see that. Merrilee was playing a Hammond C3, standing behind it in heels (painful; now *that's* professional). There is much more to her than "Angel of the Morning." She rocked the place for four hours and at the time was one of the few female headliners. She had stage presence very much like a young Bette Midler.

◄ *Poster 34a*

DECEMBER 9, 1966: KITS THEATRE

PAINTED SHIP AND THE JABBERWOCK

After six months of partners I am now back on my own. Having partners was a costly learning curve. It was not just about what it cost to buy out Roger Schiffer; it was about trust and relationships. There was a lot to be learned and as I grew up I would continue to make similar mistakes. I have been told I am too trusting, which is what my children tell me to this day. I guess I'm just a slow learner. Nevertheless I now have the dance hall back and we will see what the future has in store.

The posters just continue to improve, this one with three colours on white. You can see that Bob is coming into his own and we are both learning about the development of psychedelic posters. We know we will have to go San Francisco to check out what was going on there.

The bands for this date were two of the regulars. Roger had been quick to take on management of The Jabberwock, who would soon change their name to My Indole Ring. Thanks to me, he now had money to promote this band, which I realized I had helped in many other ways than just booking them.

We are now getting a loyal clientele at the Afterthought and they are not letting the police intimidate them.

At about this time I was fortunate to have a few "big sisters" to watch over me. These were not biological sisters, of course, but they were close friends. One of these ladies, Yvonne McKinnon, told me that sometime around 1967 a friend of hers, an Afterthought regular named Margaret, had told her she was dating a famous politician older than she was and that she wanted Yvonne to meet him. Yvonne said to bring him over to the house for a visit. A few days later I see Yvonne and ask her if there is any more to this and if she knows who the politician is. She proceeds to tell me this story.

One afternoon, Yvonne is at home with her mate, Lloyd, and their daughter, Shannon, who is a toddler, at their top-floor duplex on West Pender. They are visiting with a couple of friends in the living room, smoking a little cannabis and having a cup of tea. Lloyd notices flashing lights outside and looks out the window. There are police cars on Pender and they are blocking off all traffic on the street. As they watch, some large men get out of a sedan and start walking towards their door. They knock, open the door and start coming up the stairs. While

Poster 35 ▼

this is taking place Lloyd has grabbed the cannabis and is quickly flushing it down the toilet, which was standard practice at the time for quickly getting rid of the stuff. The men arrive at the top of the stairs and inform those present that this is not a bust, they are merely checking out the premises to make sure it is safe before their charge comes in. They quickly search the place and then go back down the stairs. Everyone is trying to figure out what is going on. Then a voice is heard at the bottom of the stairs saying, "Yvonne? It's Margaret! I have brought my friend to visit you, can we come up?" Yvonne replies, "Sure, come on up!" Up the stairs comes Margaret and right behind her is a fellow who turns out to be named Pierre Elliott Trudeau, Canada's justice minister at the time. Margaret introduces him as her fiancé and they are both invited to sit down and visit. Margaret, feeling quite at home here, is chatting away about Pierre. He seems somewhat uncomfortable with the whole situation and is very quiet. Tea is offered and declined and after a short visit Margaret and Pierre say their goodbyes, disappear down the stairs to their waiting car and are whisked away. It was shortly after this visit that the public at large learned of their relationship and, within a few years, their marriage.

DECEMBER 16, 1966: KITS THEATRE

UNCLES AL'S FANTASTIC SENSATIONS AND THE COASTMEN

One thing I know for sure was that I had a very diverse clientele ranging in age from late teens to mid-20s. I still believed that anyone in their late 20s was old and that you could not trust anyone over 30.

The hippie movement had evolved from those that were known as beatniks. Beatniks were in their late 20s, and their music of choice was folk and jazz. I had wonderful memories of this music from what I considered my youth (hey, everything is relative). So when a group came to me and said their music represented that era, I felt obliged to book them. The group was Uncle Al's Fantastic Sensations, but just to balance things I also booked the Coastmen, a much more mainstream group.

No one seems to want to take credit for this poster, especially Bob. I can

understand why, because it is not one I was particularly proud of, and for that matter neither was the event. I can only say I caved to the "seniors" of the time, who were in their late twenties. They came from the beat era so they must be right.

This poster was printed by silk screen and no one could read it, even if you were stoned. Yet another learning curve. This dance was not a success, just after things had begun to improve.

◄ *Poster 36*

DECEMBER 23 AND 26, 1966: KITS THEATRE

WILLIAM TELL & THE MARKSMEN AND TOM NORTHCOTT TRIO

DON CRAWFORD & THE RIGHT PEOPLE AND THE NORTHWEST COMPANY

Somehow I got through the last show. It was like nothing else. For the Christmas show, and last one of the year, I vowed it would be big. I arranged to have one date on the 23rd and another on the 26th. The 24th would be the first of our family's two Ukrainian Christmas Eve dinners, since not everybody was available for the traditional date on January 7. And Christmas was the 25th. The hall was not available for New Year's Eve, so I also wanted a big show for the end of the year. I booked the Tom Northcott Trio and William Tell for the Friday, while the last show of the year, on Monday the 26th, would be Don Crawford & The Right People and The Northwest Company. Don was another friend of my brother's, as he too was a folksinger. And just as with Tom Northcott, it turned out he could go from folk to rock. This lineup proved to be a great success.

The poster, again a three-colour one, was also a great hit. Today a full-colour poster would not be a big deal, but when these were being printed we had to run them through the press one colour at a time with separate negatives. Two-colour presses were new technology in those days, and my father had only a one-colour AB Dick machine. At the time, I felt we were at the cutting edge when it came to posters!

Poster 37 ▲

JANUARY 6, 1967: KITS THEATRE

UNITED EMPIRE LOYALISTS AND WINTERGREENS

It is hard to believe it's already 1967. Who knows what the new year may hold. The last dance of 1966 was a big success. I will not know for many years that I had passed up a great business opportunity with the Barnett brothers, as they would move ahead to build their business empire. I do know that all things happen for a reason, but sometimes it takes a long time to find out what that reason is. Last evening, we had a family dinner, as our oldest granddaughter, Tyesa, celebrated her 16th birthday, and by the time this book is published she will have graduated from Grade 12. She and our seven other grandchildren have taught me that lesson yet again: the reason for things takes its time to become apparent.

This poster is a really neat one and seems to have been well liked through the years.

Poster 38 ➤

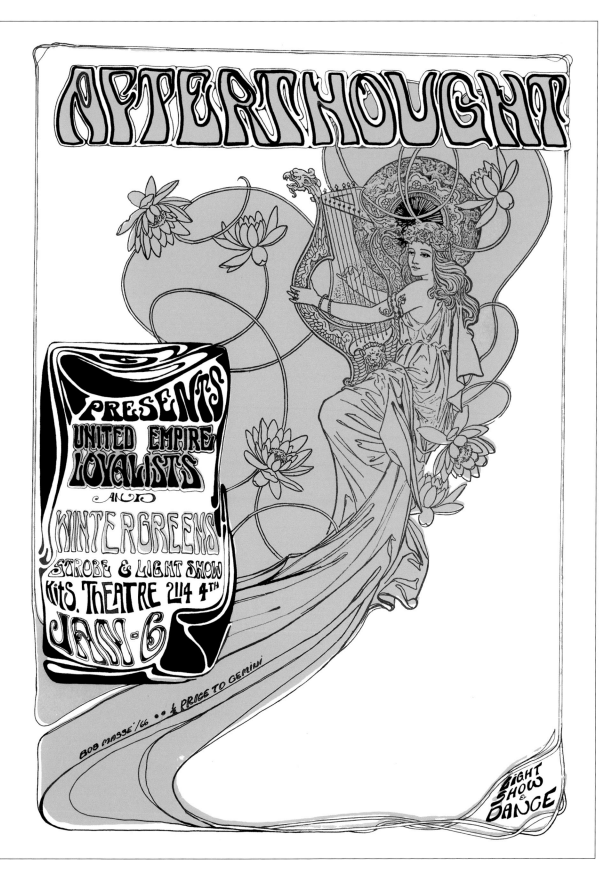

The original was the one with the white background, dated January 6. The yellow background one, poster 72, is from August 18, 1967, and the bands are United Empire Loyalists and Seeds of Time. What is puzzling is that at the time of the August event I was in Montreal and my business licence had already been revoked. So to this day I have no idea who put on this event. Also at the time, I held all the shares in Afterthought Enterprises Inc. Just another Afterthought mystery.

Winter's Green, aka Wintergreens or Wintergreen, was playing my dance hall for the first time. Bruce Allen had contacted me to book them, as he had recently started up his first agency. Winter's Green would go on to become Applejack and then Trooper, a group I think you could say did pretty well over time. They're still touring today, and I understand there is now even a tribute band for Trooper, which is surely the ultimate honour.

JANUARY 13, 1967: KITS THEATRE

SEEDS OF TIME AND UNFORESEEN

Everything is going well, as you can tell by surveying from the start until now. The posters continue to improve. One problem is I cannot put on as many shows as I would like, because I do not have enough bands. The Seeds of Time are playing for the first time. I am wondering how many customers will notice that two of the members of the band are also in William Tell & The Marksmen. Members of the Seeds of Time will go on to become Prism. It is becoming more common for musicians to play in more than one band.

I realize I need to do something to expand my band rotation. I have already done a couple of road trips to Seattle and got some great groups from the Pacific Northwest. The groups getting started in Vancouver are pretty good and will improve, but I need to expand the horizon. One thing I did not notice at the time was that many of the bands had members that were under 18. I was so preoccupied with making sure customers were of legal age that I forgot about the musicians.

Poster 39 ➤

It seemed the police overlooked it too, though, because they never checked.

My trial for possession of cannabis still lay in the future, but my lawyer, Gary Lauk, knew the legal system and managed to keep getting the trial delayed.

Actually, that was just one of the obstacles I had to deal with. Another big one was my lack of formal education. As I recall these poster stories I often wonder how I managed to keep it all going. I started off in school by failing Grade 1. When I started school I was left-handed and would write things backwards. My teachers would say I was lazy and not trying. This was not what a 6-year-old wants to hear, of course. My one vivid Grade 1 memory is getting hit on my left hand so that I would use my right instead. It took two years but I finally learned to write right-handed. By the time I got to Grade 5 I had become a tough little kid with attitude who had learned how to survive. I had formed what I thought of as my own gang. My Grade 5 teacher told me I had a bad attitude, a lack of respect, would not focus and just wanted to daydream. Besides giving me a lot of beatings, he felt that the best way to deal with me was to have me fail Grade 5. So here I am, 11 years old and being told I am lazy and no good. My mother tried to change this teacher's attitude, to no avail. His name was Jerry too, and the school dealt with his

teaching habits by promoting him to principal. This would be the end of my Catholic elementary school education. My mother enrolled me in public school, where I survived for the next couple of years. It was at this time that I discovered coffeehouses, and the rest, as they say, is history. I did go to high school, though I was absent more than I attended.

So now I am operating a successful dance hall despite my very limited formal education. Many years later I would graduate from night school and go on to college. I will never forget, at my college graduation, my daughter Celeste, then aged 4, shouting "Daddy! Daddy!" when I went up on stage to receive my diploma. That made my long struggle for education worth it.

When I was taking child psychology in college I came to understand my own childhood. Two things I believe I had as a child, and still struggle with today, are dyslexia and attention deficit disorder. It was while researching for this book that I learned that a treatment for both these disorders is Dexedrine, more commonly known as "speed." And at the peak of my operating the Afterthought, that was in fact my drug of choice because I thought it helped me focus. My close friends thought I was crazy to do as much of it as I did. If only I knew then what I know now, would things ever have been different!

JANUARY 20, 1967: KITS THEATRE

PAINTED SHIP AND WILLIAM TELL & THE MARKSMEN

I tell Bob that this poster needs to be great. He agrees, as he wants to come to San Francisco with me.

I had been talking to my friends for a while about going to San Francisco to book bands. No local bands had been able to draw the crowd the Grateful Dead did (1,000+), and I wanted that number back. I decided we would hold over this week's bands for the next weekly dance, thereby enabling us to use the same poster with an overlay. This would give me a week to get to San Francisco and back. It was agreed we would load up the car, leave once the dance got going, drive all night and be back by the following Friday to do the next event.

One small problem: I had not told Julie about this. She knew I was planning to go to San Francisco and wanted to come with me. However, I knew her parents would freak out and not let her go. This was the start of my comprehending that I was truly in love with her, but I did not yet know she was destined to be my soulmate. I realized I was doing everything I could to protect her and not allowing her to do the stupid things I was doing. I felt a strong pull to protect her. This was the start of a lifelong relationship; I just didn't know it at the time. Julie, however, was much smarter and turned out to have the patience of Job. I feel truly blessed and know now that if it weren't for her I would never have survived.

So here we go. I make sure my mother will close up the venue, and I persuade Julie to drive her home. I fill the gas tank of my Mustang convertible, load up everyone and off we go to San Francisco.

First stop, the US border. The customs officer asks the standard "where are you going?" I reply "to San Francisco to book some bands." Officer says "fine" and we are on our way. We had all agreed we would only stop for gas and washrooms and only when really needed, as we wanted to get to the Bay area as quickly as possible. I had been told by friends that I could get there in less than 24 hours. It was simple: we would take turns driving in five-hour shifts. As there were four of us, it would be easy. And it was.

So, what to do first? What things do we want to get done? I already had many invites from friends I had met at the Trips

Festival in Vancouver. Jerry Garcia had said I was always welcome at their band house, as they had recently moved into the Haight. When I talked with Janis Joplin, she too had said please come down and visit. I knew I had to see the Fillmore and the Avalon, the happening dance halls, and I had to buy a pair of Beatle boots, which you could not get in Vancouver at the time. I had been told they would be available in San Francisco. Yes, I do have a bit of a shoe fetish. I was, as far as I was concerned, slumming it by wearing jeans

◄ *Poster 40*

and T-shirts; I had left my suits behind. First thing when we arrived I found a shoe store in the heart of the city. I now have my new boots and I am happy. Next stop, the Grateful Dead's house. I knock on the door and just walk in. I am greeted by assorted band members. It seems like a homecoming. I tell them I have a few friends along and we are in town for a few days. They tell me no problem, we can all crash at their place. They tell me that Big Brother & The Holding Company are playing at the Matrix Sunday night and I should check out Janis, as she is much better than when I last saw her.

HAIGHT ASHBURY DISTRICT, SAN FRANCISCO

GRATEFUL DEAD PHOTO OPPORTUNITY

My friend Danny Kennedy is part of this road trip. I ask him if he wants to come with me to check out the Fillmore, as it is Saturday and we can go to the Matrix tomorrow. Danny is part of my original gang from elementary school. He would continue to be part of my life until he was tragically killed by someone who turned out to be a very bad product of the sixties. Danny was working for his aunt and one of his jobs was to collect rents from

her properties in Vancouver. Danny went to answer his front door one day and was greeted by a guy named Digger who proceeded to stab Danny to death, mainly because Digger could not pay his rent. Danny was a good person and I will always miss him. The casualties of the time continue to grow.

As we are going out the door a dude is coming in asking whose Mustang convertible is outside. I tell him it's mine and he says, "Cool. Can I take a picture of it with the band?" I say sure and next thing I know a photo op is happening with my car. I never thought the picture would become part of the Dead's history.

We have dinner in the Haight and then head over to the Fillmore. The Fillmore was the first dance hall I had ever been in other than my own. The group playing that night was the Paul Butterfield Blues Band.

I was looking for more of a rock sound but I knew I would see Janis the next night. I introduced myself to Bill Graham, telling him about my place in Vancouver. He was extremely nice to me, and not anything like I had been told to expect. He said I should come back on a weekday so we could spend more time when he didn't have a show to deal with. I thanked him for his time and we met later in the week as agreed.

[Figure 41] (Grateful Dead promo shot in front of Jerry's Mustang) ▼

FEBRUARY 22, 1967: THE MATRIX, SAN FRANCISCO

JANIS JOPLIN

Well I am ready for my second day in San Francisco. I leave the Dead house and grab something to eat on Haight Street. I then wander down the street to Golden Gate Park, where I am told there are some bands playing. I am blown away, as there is the smell of pot everywhere. I can't believe how out in the open everything is. I am stoned very quickly and trying to adjust to the new terrain. The rest of the day passed in a daze. I have returned to this park many times, with my own kids when they were young and later with my grandchildren.

One of my trips back to San Francisco was for the thirtieth anniversary of the Summer of Love and Be-In. We went with our daughter Celeste and her husband, Dale. While they and Julie sat and enjoyed the music I wandered off. I was warmly greeted by Chet Helms and was invited backstage to meet the bands. It was if time had stood still. As I continued to return to the park for various events I still would get flashbacks.

It is now Sunday evening and we are on the way to the Matrix, at a great location close to San Francisco Bay. At the door I ask for Janis and she greets me like I was an old friend. I introduce her to Danny and she shows us to her table at the back of the club. She says she is about to start her set and will visit with us during her breaks. The first set finishes and she comes back to the table with a bottle of Southern Comfort. This was my first introduction to this wonder drink, which would become Julie's favourite as well. We had a wonderful evening and Janis would tell me I need to bring her group back to Vancouver. I would not commit to this, as it is only my second night in San Francisco. When her show finished she wanted to give me the poster you see overleaf. She offered to sign it and I said no, it's okay, but I will take the poster. I say good night and tell her we need to crash, as we have just driven straight through from Vancouver. She says cool, and we leave. Danny then says to me, "You know, she was hitting on you." I then realized how much I love Julie and that I was missing her. This evening would be the last time I would see Janis Joplin alive. It was

BIG BROTHER AND THE HOLDING COMPANY

JAN 17 TUES JAN 22 SUN • VIVA • SANTANA • SAN FRANCISCO

1936 FILLMORE • 567-9118

MINORS WELCOME

a wonderful evening and she was much too young when she died at 27. When I returned home I gave the poster to Julie and she has kept it for all these years.

◄ *Poster 42*

FEBRUARY 22, 1967: THE MATRIX, SAN FRANCISCO

STEVE MILLER

Sometime during the course of that same evening, I met Steve Miller, who introduced himself as an up-and-coming blues player. His band had done the Matrix the previous week, so he gave me a poster that was still hanging up at the club. He too offered to sign it, and again I said no. I gave this poster too to Julie, the one you see overleaf. I obviously did not have a good appreciation for the value of an autograph. It could have had something to do with being eighteen years old and my huge ego. I would meet Steve later in the week and come to an agreement to book him for my dance hall. Steve told me to call his band the Steve Miller Blues Band from Chicago. When I asked why not San Francisco he said I would draw more people if I said he was from Chicago. We agreed on a date and negotiated a fee of $500, as that is what I had paid the Grateful Dead.

The next day was a visit to the Fillmore to meet with Bill Graham. He invites me into his office and it was a meeting I will never forget. I believed then and still do to this day that he was the godfather of rock and roll promoters. He sat at his desk and I sat opposite him. As he spoke I felt like I was listening to someone who understood what I was trying to do with my dance hall. He gave me a lot of good advice. I realized that we were running our dance halls in a very similar manner other than the fact that he used people instead of German shepherds for security. He agreed I should book Steve Miller and Country Joe & The Fish. He advised me against booking Janis, as he felt she was too much of a stoner and that I would not be able to rely on her. I took his advice, but I did find it interesting that a short time later he would sign her and her group to an exclusive contract. To my surprise it was not until I read

Graham's biography that I discovered how straight he really was and that he was in his thirties when we had that first meeting. He was my mentor and I am proud to have known him, even if he was that old.

Next stop was at the Avalon Ballroom to meet Chet Helms. Chet was much younger than Graham and much more casual. He proceeded to tell me the difference in how he worked as compared to Bill. I did not know at the time that they had worked together when they first started. In the end I felt a closer alliance with Bill than with Chet, but they were both good people who died sooner than they should have. When researching for this book I discovered that we all started in the business at about the same time: same month, same year.

It is now 46 years later. I am again in San Francisco, visiting family this time, and I receive an email from Matt Laundrie, a young Victoria promoter. He tells me he has confirmed Steve Miller for a concert on July 30, 2013. I returned home in April looking forward to helping Matt in any way possible, and was asked to get involved with promotion of the event. One of my ideas was to reprint the postcard from the time I first booked Steve Miller, and to give one away with every ticket sold. We would also give away restored reproductions of the original poster on The Q, 100.3 FM, the Victoria radio station promoting the event.

◄ *Poster 43*

While talking with John Shields from The Q, I pointed out I was the first one to bring Steve Miller to Canada. John joked that this could be his last concert in Canada (sort of matching bookends). However, judging from the success of the concert, I think not. The show was held in Esquimalt at their local arena called the Archie Browning Sports Centre. The staff there were wonderful and I believe they were an important part of what made the show such a great success.

After the sound check I was able to give Steve a copy of the original Afterthought poster. He seemed pleased. I then told him about the book I was writing. As we were talking he saw the original poster he had given me in San Francisco all those years ago and he offered to sign it again. This time I said thank you with great appreciation. He also offered to sign the original artwork for his appearance at the Afterthought. I now have two autographed Steve Miller posters. Steve is a wonderful person and I trust he will continue to entertain his many fans for many years to come.

While I was writing this postscript I was being entertained by three of my grandsons during a family reunion. After much noise and hijinks, quiet reigned again and I heard my grandson Blair playing my brother's guitar oh so softly. It took me back in an instant. I still miss Terry after all these years.

FEBRUARY 23, 1967: BERKELEY, CALIFORNIA

BANANA POWER

I am now on my way to Berkeley to Ed Denson's house. Ed is the manager of Country Joe & The Fish. I am not sure when I first heard the band – maybe at Golden Gate Park. I think they have a great sound and I really want to be the first to bring them to Canada. This is the one band I do not hear any negatives about; they are just a good group. Joe has something special when he is on stage. So I think it is really neat that I have an invite to their manager's place for lunch to discuss booking the band.

I find the house in Berkeley, which is a feat unto itself, and I am greeted at the door by Ed. We go into the living room and have a seat on the floor. Ed says Joe will be here shortly but we should decide on the dates and fees. I tell Ed I pay out-of-town groups $500, as that is what I had paid the Grateful Dead. As we are discussing possible dates, Joe walks in the door with a beautiful girl on each arm and carrying a bunch of bananas. I think this looks cool, of course, but why the bananas? As I am trying to be cool, I just say hello to Joe. He responds with "Good to see you" and says he'll be with us in a few

minutes, as he has to do something for us. I continue talking with Ed about the gig and I hear a lot of noise coming from the kitchen. My curiosity is getting the best of me! I want to know what is going on, so I excuse myself to go to the washroom. I return through the kitchen, where I see Joe and the girls scraping off the insides of the banana peels. Naturally, I am not going to ask what they are doing, because of course I'm much too cool for that. So I return to my meeting with Ed. We continue to talk and are now discussing multiple dates. How cool is that? The next thing I see is Joe and his friends coming into the room. Joe is carrying what appears to be a pile of joints on a tray. One of the girls has wine glasses, the other a bottle of wine.

(At this time in my life, as I have said before, I spent most of my time stoned. Being stoned was normal for me and it would continue to get worse. But I would have to learn this the hard way, because I would not listen to anyone. I was convinced I knew it all, as I was a successful rock promoter.)

Poster 44 ➤

THE GOLDEN SHEAF BAKERY PRESENTS   IN BERKELEY

DANCE-CONCERT

JANUARY
6 13 14
8 PM
1.75 ADV.
2.00 DOOR

COUNTRY JOE AND THE FISH
THE WILDFLOWER
JOHN FAHEY
LIGHTS BY BILL HAM AND CO.

PLUS
FILMS BY
ROBERT
NELSON

FINNISH BROTHERHOOD HALL

CHESTNUT JUST OFF UNIVERSITY

TICKETS: A.S.U.C., MOES, SHAKESPEARE & CO., DISCOUNT RECORDS, IN BERKELEY
PSYCHEDELIC SHOP, CITY LIGHTS, IN SAN FRANCISCO

THE GOLDEN SHEAF BAKERY PRESENTS   IN BERKELEY

Back to the meeting: the girls and Joe sit on the floor. Someone pours the wine and Joe lights up what I think is a joint. He inhales and passes it on. As I take it I notice it does not smell like pot. Joe tells me it is not pot but the dried inside peel of bananas. Joe then says, "You'll like it. It's a cool high." I am thinking "yes, this is a cool high." After we finish the wine and smoke a lot of banana joints we finalize the fees and dates for Country Joe's performances in Vancouver. I say my goodbyes. Joe pulls me aside and tells me the whole banana thing is a hoax but I can't tell anyone, because he is going to introduce the banana high idea at my dance hall to see what happens. The rest is history and all that, including Donovan's 1966 hit song "Mellow Yellow." Except I later learned from Joe's drummer, Chicken Hirsh, that all of this took place in Vancouver and not in San Francisco!

COUNTRY JOE & THE FISH

FEEL-LIKE-I'M-FIXIN'-TO-DIE RAG

As I am leaving Ed Denson's place, Joe asks if I could come back in and pick up a couple of boxes of their first recording. Joe tells me it would help if we Canadians knew who the group were before they arrived, if some of their music was being played. He then tells me there is one small problem: I would have to smuggle the records into Canada, for reasons that to this day I do not understand. I still agreed to take the records and said I would find a store to sell them and get some airplay on the local stations. I put the boxes in the trunk of my car and returned to the Dead's house in San Francisco.

The records made it safely to Vancouver and were sold at a couple of local stores: the Psychedelic Shop and the Record Gallery. They were kept under the counter and you had to ask for them by name before you could purchase any. They would be handed to you in a plain brown bag.

I talked to my friends and we figured out that we would have to leave on Thursday in order to be back in Vancouver for my Friday night dance. This gave me one more day to be a tourist. It seems the rest of my friends had already been tourists. We got up the next morning, a Wednesday, and set off to see the local sights – over the Golden Gate Bridge to Sausalito to see as much of the

Poster 45 (composite) ➤

108

Country Joe

Bay area as we could. Thursday arrives in the blink of an eye, it seems, and we must be off. We say our goodbyes. Danny and Pigpen, the drummer for Grateful Dead, seem to have become good friends. As they are saying goodbye, neither knows that this will be the last time they will see each other, as Pigpen would die at the age of 27.

We drive across the Bay bridge and head for USC Berkeley, as I want to do some shopping and compare the campus to the University of Washington in Seattle. I had never attended university but I liked the energy on campus. Next stop is Ed's house again, where we take the boxes of records out of the trunk and stash them under the back seat amongst the springs. Who knew how easy it was to get the back seat out of a Mustang?! We say more goodbyes and it's off to the freeway. It is now Thursday afternoon and we have to be in Vancouver by tomorrow afternoon to set up for that evening's show.

JANUARY 27, 1967: KITS THEATRE

PAINTED SHIP AND WILLIAM TELL & THE MARKSMEN

The last six days have been a blur except for the encounters described above. I do believe I was fortunate to get home. We knew we did not have a lot of time; we had to drive straight back, no delays. As we approached our first mountain pass we see a sign saying all vehicles must have tire chains when there is snow in the pass. What snow? We are in California. It doesn't snow here! Well, we found out it does indeed snow in the mountain passes. We pull into a gas station and they tell us the price for chains. We do not have enough money between us. I have enough for gas and our basic needs. California was a lot more expensive than we thought it would be. Interac and credit cards didn't exist yet, or if they did I didn't know about them. So, what to do? Danny approaches the gas station attendant and says how about a trade for my watch. This was not just any watch, but his grandfather's watch which Danny had received as a gift. I am blown away. I tell Danny, "You can't do this." His response was, "Do you have a better idea? And do you want to get back in time to

Poster 46 ➤

open your dance hall?" Of course, there is no other solution. We finally get back on the road and now we are really moving, for it is already Friday afternoon. We are getting closer to the border but realize we are still not in Vancouver like we should be by now.

I decide to phone Terry. I am reluctant to do so, as sadly I have learned not to rely on him because of his major drug problems. (As if I could talk about that!) But he says, "Don't worry, I can take care of it, little brother." I am nervous but have no other choice. We start to approach the border. Again I am nervous. I have never smuggled records or anything else into the country before. I think to myself, "I am out on bail. What will happen if I get busted again?" We approach the border and they ask, "Where have you been?" We tell them, "California, on business." "Anything to declare?" Everyone rattles off different things. I tell them about my Beatle boots. The officer says, "Fine, carry on." Huge sigh of relief and we are back in Canada. We get to the dance hall in the evening and I am greeted by Julie, my mom and my brother. Everything is going well. The band is playing, light show is working, security is in place, all is well. I think to myself how grateful I am that this is a dance held over by popular demand. It would be the first and last one where I was able to use the old "back by popular demand" trick.

FEBRUARY 3, 1967: KITS THEATRE

UNITED EMPIRE LOYALISTS AND UNFORESEEN

I am on a roll again. The last dance was a great success. This poster is Bob Masse's first move to a larger format. Up until now all his posters for the Afterthought had been either 4¼ × 11, 8½ × 11 or 8½ × 14. Everyone liked the larger-format poster on card stock. Bob was well on his way to developing this, creating his second, even larger poster right after finishing the first. It is very obvious how much he has been influenced by meeting fellow designers in San Francisco. It would not take long for this bigger size to become the norm for posters. Look closely at this one and see if you can figure out where the design was used for a recreated poster at an earlier date.

Poster 47 ➤

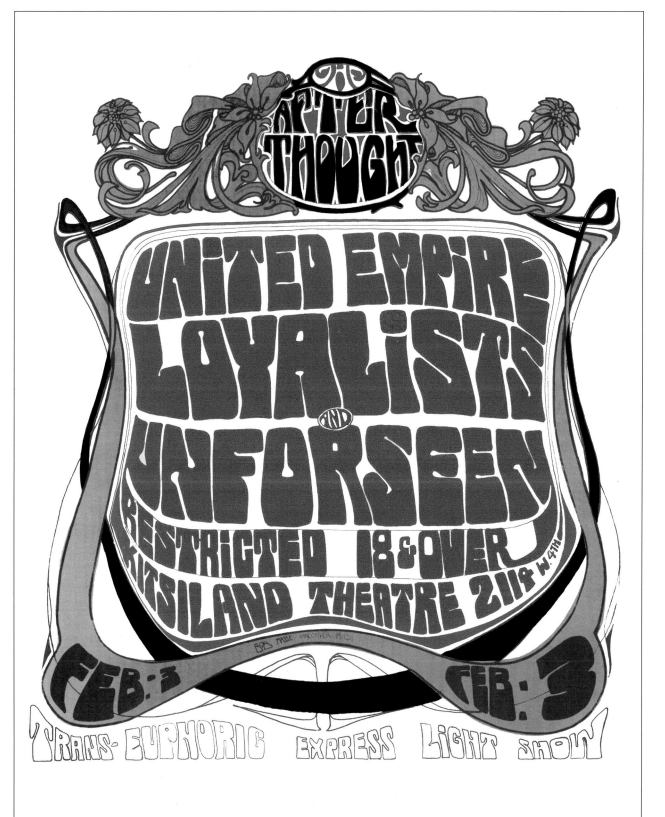

THE AFTER THOUGHT

UNITED EMPIRE LOYALISTS AND UNFORSEEN

RESTRICTED 18 & OVER

KITSILAND THEATRE 2114 W. 4TH

BPS MADE VANCOUVER B.C.

FEB. 3   FEB. 3

TRANS-EUPHORIC EXPRESS LIGHT SHOW

So here we are at the end of the night, and Danny Tripper, Danny Mack and Danny Kennedy come to me after the show and tell me about a great party they have been invited to. They say we should all go. I say sure. So we all pile into my Mustang. Here I am with the three Dannys in the car and I say where is the party? They reply it's in Banff, Alberta, only a 12-hour drive, tops. Sure, why not. We'd had a good weekend, I had lots of money, let's go. So off to Banff we went. I didn't consider that it was the middle of winter and that there could be snow, but of course we would not run into any. I remember going over Vancouver's Port Mann bridge and thinking how big and cool it was. Onward to Banff, only ten hours to go.

(Flash forward 48 years and I am going over the new Port Mann bridge on my way to meet a dear old friend, Theresa "Bitty" Neel, who is now living in Chilliwack. She is now a native elder, but back in the day she used to put up posters for me. I reflected on bridging the passage of so much time.)

This trip to Banff was insane from the start and as I think about it now I realize how fortunate I am that I survived it. So many crazy adventures that I somehow made it through. But back to the trip at hand – and I do mean trip! – we arrived in Banff in the wee hours and the party was still going. I am not sure how long it went on after we got there but I believe it was several days. Partied out, we got back in the car for the return trip. I still have a vivid memory of that icy road and the front of my Mustang sliding under the back of a semi as the truck moved forward. Talk about a life-threatening moment and I am still alive to talk about it. Must have been a lot of guardian angels that day.

Somehow we managed to get back to Vancouver with all of us unharmed. Both Danny Tripper and Danny Mack were members of what I thought was a great band, Fireweed. They would both go on to be recognized musicians in their own right. Danny Tripper has since passed away. He will be remembered.

I have continued to push the envelope in taking chances with my life. I had experienced many traumas in my youth, and looking back, I just wish I had been able to deal with my numerous issues. Instead I attempted to bury them by staying stoned and trying to fit in. Peer pressure can be an amazingly strong force, especially if you don't even know it's happening.

FEBRUARY 10, 11, 1967: KITS THEATRE

MARTHA MUSHROOM'S FANTASTIC SENSATIONS AND UNITED EMPIRE LOYALISTS

PAINTED SHIP AND MARTHA MUSHROOM'S FANTASTIC SENSATIONS

I decide to go for two nights, as I have a chance to book what I believe is a great new band, Martha Mushroom's Fantastic Sensations. And I book them for both nights because I know they have a great following.

This poster is in three colours on white card stock. Neither Bob nor I had thought of doing one any bigger than 11 × 17 before, simply because I was making them all in my father's print shop, which could not handle anything larger at the time. But Bob wanted bigger after seeing the posters in San Francisco for the Avalon and the Fillmore. This seemed reasonable. I was making money and could afford to pay a different printer. We found a shop in New Westminster called Playwright Printers. It was very strange to go elsewhere, as my father had done all of our posters to date except for the two that were silk screened (an idea that did not work for us). I had always had a rocky relationship with my father and I was not sure how he would react. I put it to him this way: it was

business and he could not print the size we wanted.

Interestingly enough, my father's former shop, Dominion Printers, is now known as Metro Printers, owned by Mike Kyer, a very close friend who I think of as a little brother. The printing industry has changed so much over the past forty-plus years. Everything today can be printed at one place.

I now have my first large poster in what I think of as full colour. It is just like the ones I'd brought back from San Francisco for Julie, none of which I got autographed even though the performers always offered to. If only I had known. But at least Julie saved them all. She always did the right things and was always there for me. It blows my mind how stupid I was in not listening to her at the time. I always thought I knew best, but I would have a lot more to learn and had no idea of how rocky the road ahead would be.

I now have just one week to put on a huge show with Country Joe & The Fish, who are arriving from San Francisco.

◀ *Poster 48*

FEBRUARY 16–18, 1967

COUNTRY JOE & THE FISH

This is the big event I have wanted to do for a long time. I'd hung out with Country Joe & The Fish in San Francisco and I have a different band to open for each of three nights. Bob Masse really outdid himself with this poster. He had a lot of lead time and had been with me when I booked Country Joe. I thought this poster with the illustration of the band was his best one yet, and certainly the biggest.

Everything was set to go. I remember the opening night of Country Joe very clearly because when they did their sound check earlier in the day they'd played "Sweet Lorraine," a beautiful song. It was a tune ahead of its time, with a lot of bells and different sounds not usually heard in music anyone else was doing then. Much as I liked the song, I started to worry that patrons might not dance to it, as it was so far out. The band opened with "Sweet Lorraine" that night and I stood against the wall feeling very nervous about how the crowd would react. But I soon got over that, because it was magical to see everyone start swaying in time to the music. I

knew then the date would be a success, a night never to forget.

When the band came back on after their first break Joe was carrying a bunch of bananas. He proceeded to tell the audience how you could get high on the inside scrapings of banana peels. He explained the process in great detail, telling them how to prepare the banana skins for smoking. While this was going on, the band was drinking from a pitcher of something, which I later found out was laced with LSD. The concerts were fantastic, each night better than the last.

This first show of Country Joe & The Fish in Canada will always be remembered for the bananas. It did not take long before there was a shortage of bananas in Greater Vancouver, and when the band returned to San Francisco and told the banana story again, one was hard pressed to find a banana in the Bay area either. Joe was right when he first told me this would happen. They were a fantastic band and we had a wonderful weekend.

While doing the research for this book, though, I discovered that I did not

FROM SAN FRANCISCO

COUNTRY JOE AND TH FISH

ALSO PLAYING AT COUNTRY JOE FEST

FOR 3 DAYS!

THURS. 16

FRIDAY 17

SAT. 18

AFTERTHOUGHT

TICKET OUTLETS: PSYCHEDELIC SHOP · RECORD GALLERY · DOWNSTAIRS GALLERY (Village Square)
VANCOUVER B.C.   ADVANCED: 2.50 / DOOR: 3.00

© 2006 Bob Masse

provide accommodations for Country Joe & The Fish, because they never asked me to. Yet, when I'd booked the Grateful Dead the previous summer, Jerry Garcia had told me I had to provide rooms. And of course I complied, but as mentioned earlier, the motel was not the greatest. I now realize I have no memory at all of providing accommodation for any of the bands. You have to realize I was not exactly working from some manual on how psychedelic promoters are supposed to do things, and band billeting was not something my mentors ever covered.

It came time to say our goodbyes to Country Joe & The Fish. Everyone wanted them to come back. I agreed and made a deal for them to return in a few weeks. I must have done something right, as they were willing to come back, lack of accommodations notwithstanding. I am told the band just crashed in houses in the neighbourhood and that a lot of partying went on that weekend, parties that are still talked about to this day.

◄ *Poster 49*

FEBRUARY 24, 1967: KITS THEATRE

JOE MOCK & NO COMMERCIAL POTENTIAL AND THE JABBERWOCK

Joe Mock is another old friend from the folk music scene. Joe had seen Tom Northcott, Don Crawford and others try out rock and roll and thought why not? Thus was a new band born: Joe Mock & No Commercial Potential. Joe remains a good friend, who now lives with his family in the south of France. He still returns to BC once a year and tours with Pied Pear (also called Pied Pumkin [sic]) and with Mock Duck, two bands he formed after No Commercial Potential. A good lifestyle.

This 12 × 18 poster would be Bob Masse's first full-colour one for me and I believe it's the first full-colour work he ever produced for a dance hall. I feel safe in this statement, as the Afterthought was the only psychedelic dance hall in greater Vancouver at the time.

This time in my life was getting more and more difficult. On one side I had this big, booming dance hall business where the sky was the limit, but looming on the other side was my trial date on the pot charge. If

convicted, I was facing jail time, but more important I would be forced to close the dance hall because as a convicted felon I would not be able to have a licence to operate. The thought of this was creating a very deep depression in me. What should I do? Of course, get stoned more often. The fact of the matter is that I was stoned more than I was straight. My brother was using a lot of heroin at this time; in fact he was wired to the teeth. But he would not acknowledge his serious drug problem. He would tell me to try the stuff and assured me it would take the edge off my stress. After a lot of pressure and watching Terry use this forbidden drug I decided to try it with him just this one time. When he injected me it was unbelievable. No longer did I feel any pain or stress. He assured me I would not get addicted if I only "chipped at it," meaning use it only once in a while.

There is a very strong view out there that cannabis leads to hard drug use. I do not believe this is true. What I think led to my hard-drug use was depression. And what led to my depression at the time was the impending trial for possession of less than half an ounce of cannabis. It seems to me that society must understand that when someone feels they need to use something to alter their consciousness, the problem is why they need to alter their consciousness in the first place. The drug roller coaster I had been riding for a while now was about to take some very serious ups and downs. If only I had known then where I was going!

The use of hard drugs would take me to dark places. The fact is that all illegal street drugs bring forth an element in people that causes them to have no care for humankind and they will do whatever it takes to get what they want. I once witnessed someone get shot in the leg with a gun only because the shooter asked him where he wanted to get shot. It really was "strange days." The person who got shot was being put through law school by a very serious drug dealer who thought it would be good to have a lawyer on his team and in his control. I am sure he would not be the first or the last lawyer to be bought by organized crime. My conclusion was that if you declare something illegal, you will soon get organized crime around it. You'd think we would have figured this out with liquor prohibition! Suffice to say the "war on drugs" has been going on for over half a century and it's still a stalemate.

◀ *Poster 50*

MARCH 3, 4, 1967

CARNIVAL AND WILLIAM TELL & THE MARKSMEN
CARNIVAL AND SEEDS OF TIME

Poster 53 is one of five full-size ones in multiple colours – superb work by Bob Masse, really coming into his own as a top designer. He would go on to be recognized the world over for his poster art. I have known Bob for close to 50 years and he continues to create great posters for globally recognized groups.

Around the time this one was done, I'd mentioned to Bob that I had heard from Country Joe & The Fish when they were here that there was buzz in the business that Bob was just copying the poster art of San Francisco. Never mind that the Haight designers themselves were pretty shamelessly copying much earlier work, such as by Czech artist Alphonse Mucha (1860–1939), as shown in posters 51 and 52 next page. I believe Bob did not take this criticism lightly, and his response was the Afterthought poster you see here. I think he was subtly telling the Avalon show's promoter, Family Dog, to "suck on this": note the difference in what the lady's thumb is pointing to in posters 52 and 53.

But never mind all that. The point of contention for me in Bob's poster was what looked like a hash pipe. I felt I was in enough trouble already, with police doing everything they could to close me down. They clearly had their orders from "Tom Terrific" Campbell, Vancouver's mayor at the time, to clean up Fourth Avenue!

In the end, I would not be able to continue, because of my earlier bust, and the city would succeed in closing me down. A real "afterthought," and a vindication of sorts, would occur some forty years later when Julie and I were invited to the opening of a new exhibit at the Vancouver Museum profiling the history of the city and of course including the sixties. In the exhibit are Afterthought posters plus a short history of the dance hall. I found it very interesting, and I could see nothing negative about the display. It was fascinating to see the many ways history can be communicated.

During the reception at the opening of the new exhibit, Senator Larry Campbell came up to me and introduced himself. I felt honoured to meet him. As I remember it, he proceeded to tell me that in

Poster 53 ➤

Poster 51 ▲

Poster 52 ➤

his youth, when he was in the RCMP, he and his fellow officers would attend the Afterthought as undercover officers in order to bust my customers. It seems this was a special police detail who all lived in a house in North Vancouver and were attempting together to clean up the city. I cannot help but wonder about the cost to the RCMP and the use of tax dollars. What is most interesting, though, is that

Senator Campbell is now one of a group of VIPs trying to have cannabis decriminalized. According to his webpage, he was also instrumental in getting the InSite legal safe injection initiative started. It is indeed fascinating what changes can happen given enough time. We can only hope and pray that our prime minister after 2015 will listen to Canadians and change the present cannabis laws.

MARCH 17, 18, 19, 1967: KITS THEATRE

STEVE MILLER BLUES BAND AND THE COLLECTORS

This poster was conceived on a napkin in a coffee shop at Fourth and Arbutus that is still operating to this day. Bob Masse and I had met there and I told him I had an idea for a poster. I knew I was quite stoned and I wasn't too sure about Bob. My idea was to have an old man with an exploding face. I thought it would be extra cool. And I watched Bob draw my concept right there on that napkin. It was amazing. Then he went home and created a masterpiece. It would come to be published many years later in a book of posters called *The Art of Rock: Posters from Presley to Punk*, by Paul Grushkin, as an excellent example of what is now known as psychedelic art.

The headliner was the Steve Miller Blues Band. As mentioned earlier, I had met Steve in San Francisco. I did not know where he was from, but he insisted he wanted to be billed as being from Chicago. He thought that would be a better draw than saying he was from San Francisco.

The Collectors were from Vancouver and were originally called the Classics, a local R&B band performing on the high school circuit. They were at the time the house band for a strip club called the Torch.

I must confess that this was the club I went to on Thursday nights even though I was only 18 and the age for admission to licensed places was 21. The band played mainly cover tunes and did a great job. Their manager, Jim Wisbey, who later became a physiotherapist in LA, also handled both Tom Northcott and the Classics. Jim said I should book the Classics into my dance hall. He said they had a new name, The Collectors, and had just released a new tune called "Looking at a Baby" that would soon top the charts. He went on to tell me that if I booked them he did not want me to tell anyone they were a Canadian band. Back then if you wanted to make it to the big time you needed to be from the USA; a band would have a strike against it if it was Canadian. Wisbey told me he would rent some billboards in town that would say only "The Collectors are coming." This sounded like a cool idea. We agreed they would open for the Steve Miller Blues Band. I thought this was a fantastic lineup, with both bands playing for the first time in Canada. The next day, the local buzz was about how great these two new bands were. I felt it was ironic, as

125

all the musicians from both bands had already been playing for years. I have often wondered how different the show would have been if everyone knew the real history of both of these groups.

This poster is the only one where I kept the original, hand-drawn artwork. It has always hung proudly in our home. Over the years, when people have seen it they have always asked about the story behind it. This poster would also turn out to be the last large-format one for the Afterthought. I just didn't know that at the time.

◄ *Poster 55*
Posters 57a, 57b ▼

▲ *Posters 54, 56*

MARCH 21–26, 1967: SFU, UBC, KITS THEATRE, EASTER BE-IN AT STANLEY PARK

COUNTRY JOE & THE FISH AND UNITED EMPIRE LOYALISTS

I remember the day so well: Country Joe and his band getting off the plane from San Francisco. I loved this band, not just for their music but for what they stood for. I feel they were instrumental in helping to stop the US war on Vietnam with their famous hit "I Feel Like I'm Fixin' to Die Rag."

Poster 58 ➤

When I greeted them, Joe handed me a package and told me it was time I should be recognized. He knew that Bill Graham was my mentor, that I considered myself fortunate to have met such a great impresario, and that I tried to follow Bill's example in how he put shows together. I opened the box and saw it was filled with posters. Joe on his own had had a poster designed for his week of shows in Vancouver, and in the top left-hand corner was my name. I was blown away. Joe said that if Graham could put his name on posters, so could I.

This is the reason there are two posters for this event. Bob Masse had chosen a different format from what he had been doing, and that version included only the three Kits Theatre dates. Yet somehow, in my subconscious, I felt that the end of the Afterthought was near.

Country Joe were and still are a great band, and forty-plus years later (minus guitarist Barry "The Fish" Melton) they would come back to Vancouver to do a benefit for me. At the time, I was helping Peter Barnett with his Sunshine Wheels

society, a charity that was sending bicycles to developing countries (see poster 87 opposite page 188). The Country Joe Band, as they are now called, did two concerts, in Vancouver and Victoria. An interesting footnote would be that Joe said Victoria reminded him of what Vancouver was like in the sixties.

At the Victoria show there were a lot of friends and family in the audience who knew nothing of my past. Joe talked a bit onstage about when I was a young kid in Vancouver. He told the crowd he could not understand how I could be put in jail for possession of two joints of cannabis, that it was a travesty. At the time, though, I still could not talk openly about being busted so long ago, when I was living my other life, the one I'd tried so hard to forget. Joe helped me that night by making me aware that I had nothing to be embarrassed about. What happened back then was something that was done to me for doing things I thought were okay: operating a dance hall and being able to smoke a joint, neither of which was hurting anyone.

◄ *Poster 59*

MARCH 26, 1967: EASTER BE-IN AT STANLEY PARK

COUNTRY JOE & THE FISH

The first time Country Joe performed for me, a group of people I considered to be on the left of the hippie movement asked me if, when I brought Country Joe back again, the band could also perform at something called a Be-In that they intended to put on in Stanley Park. The first Be-In had happened in San Francisco's Golden Gate Park and was a great success. I knew this because I had attended one of the later ones there. I thought to myself this would be a great idea, as I would get a lot of free publicity for the Afterthought.

I phoned Joe, and as expected he agreed the band would volunteer to perform in the park in addition to their solid week of appearances in Vancouver, first at Simon Fraser University, then UBC, then the three nights at the Afterthought. This would be the first and last time the Afterthought would do so many consecutive shows, and yes they were all successful.

Everything was gearing up for the Be-In. One of my good friends, Ron Ulmer, who was doing light shows for me, told me about how he got most of the equipment for the Be-In from Simon Fraser University, where he was a student. Apparently, all he

had to do was ask. And that was only one example of how the Be-In just continued to grow and take on a life of its own. I believe it also helped that Joe and the band were hanging out in Kits and doing a lot of meeting and greeting and of course continued to talk about the wonders of banana power.

Next were the Afterthought shows, which were all great and had lots more banana power.

The day of the Be-In arrived. Everyone I knew was there and it was reported to be a fantastic success! When it came time for me to go, though, I froze, terrified of getting busted again. I was suffering from enough paranoia already. So I opted to just drive around the park with my mother. All in all, what should have been the experience of a lifetime turned into another scary episode. Julie told me later she had spent her time at the Be-In looking for me, and to this day she does not understand why I was not there. I never could give a logical reason, and to be honest I am still sorry I missed the first Be-In in Stanley Park, which I was fortunate to have played a part in setting up. The good news is that the Be-In became a regular event and continued for many years after that. [In the Related Reading and Viewing section, see the CBC TV item "Hippie Youth: Vancouver's Human Be-in"; and the Dave Watson article "Vancouver Easter Be-In" from the *Georgia Straight*.]

I would like to think the event helped set the scene for Vancouver to become known as a city of peace. In later years I did attend some Be-Ins in the park, but I knew it would never be the same as being at the very first one. What I find most interesting is that the banana story continued to be talked about and appears to have taken on a life of its own. There are even more variations of the tale out there now. The Internet is good for that.

APRIL 7, 8, 1967: KITS THEATRE

UNITED EMPIRE LOYALISTS AND UNFORESEEN

UNFORESEEN AND WILLIAM TELL & THE MARKSMEN

The memory of this weekend still brings back a quick depression. I knew this would be the last Afterthought dance I would be doing on my own. The next week was my trial for possession of less than a half ounce of cannabis. If found guilty I could be facing jail time or at least probation. Many of my friends were in fact doing jail time for simple possession. The City and the police were on a crusade to save Vancouver. They really believed this, which is all the more strange given what is going on now. After more than sixty successful concerts I was very afraid of what lay ahead. So ironic that the band I booked for both nights was called the Unforeseen

This poster was back to the small format and one colour, just like when I started. I did not think it was a particularly great poster nor did I even care at the time. It is interesting to note that when Bob Masse first put up his website, he only had a few Afterthought examples and he listed this one as being his first Afterthought work. I contacted him at the time and let him know it was not the first, but the last. I also told him I had many more originals which he could scan and put up on his site. It was good to see Bob when he came over, and he was able to scan many of these other originals. It is unfortunate that I do not have all the Afterthought posters, but at least I have most of them.

MAY 10, 1967: HAPPENING AND PAINT-IN AT DANTE'S INFERNO

BOBBY TAYLOR AND THE VANCOUVERS

This poster is one I had nothing to do with. The reason I include it here is because I attended the event and took a copy of the poster for Julie, to keep up what was now a tradition to make sure to get her a poster for every event I went to.

I was at the Happening at the request of Harry Ornest. Somehow he had found out I had just been released from jail (and that fact didn't seem to bother him). He wanted me to run the Teenage Fair at the PNE for him again, only this time it was to be held in the Armoury in Kitsilano. Same pay as before: $100 a day plus expenses. This was a good deal, and boy did I need the money. Harry told me he wanted me to make sure I booked Bobby Taylor and the Vancouvers. He felt guitarist Tommy Chong had great potential and was sure Tommy would make it big someday. It seems that Harry had it right. Who knew at the time that Tommy Chong would go on to make many great albums and movies with Cheech Marin. What I found so strange was how they reflected the crazy lifestyle of Vancouver

in those days. [See Related Reading at "Tommy Chong" for a magazine article about the Vancouver scene.]

(Flash forward to our fifteenth wedding anniversary: Julie and I are on vacation in Maui and decide to go see *Still Smokin'*. In the movie there is a scene where the characters are puffing Maui Wowie. I looked around and it felt like most of the theatre was toking up. I thought about how times had changed and how right Harry had been that Tommy Chong was destined to become famous.)

It was also around this time in the spring of '67 that another figure who would become a defining part of the Vancouver scene crossed my path, totally by chance. Though the Afterthought was no more, I was still using my office in the building. And one rainy Friday afternoon as I stepped outside for a break, there was this fellow handing out newspapers under the shelter of the theatre marquee. I took a copy and we started to chat. When we exchanged names I learned I was talking to

HAPPENING
and PAINT IN
DANTE'S INFERNO
1024 DAVIE
BOBBY TAYLOR
AND THE VANCOUVERS
LIGHT SHOW
WED MAY 10
8:00
ADMISSION FREE
TO PARTICIPANTS

Dan McLeod, the publisher of this brand new biweekly called the *Georgia Straight*. Now, as mentioned earlier, I was pretty depressed about the recent loss of my dance hall business, but as we talked I could see Dan's depression trumped mine. He told me that no one in town was willing to print the next edition of his paper and he did not know what to do. I told him my father had a print shop and that I was confident he would take on the job. Fortunately I had just put back together my somewhat rocky relationship with my dad. And my father did indeed print the next edition of the *Straight*, even though his shop was not equipped to handle a newspaper efficiently. Still, printing this single issue gave Dan the time he needed to find a printer on Vancouver Island. Years later, while writing this book, I had lunch with Dan and asked if it would be okay to tell this story. His response: "Of course it's okay. My paper was always about printing the truth."

I guess you could say my truth is that this part of my life was the most difficult I had ever faced and I feel blessed to have survived it. So what happened? Well, at my trial for marijuana possession, the judge found me guilty and jailed me for three weeks while a pre-sentence report was prepared. This is difficult to write about, because other than to Julie I have never talked about it. I was terrified, to say the least. I was taken back to

◄ *Poster 61*

a holding cell, which held very bad memories for me from my last experience. It was back to being searched: just a brief frisk this time, though with more to come. I was then put into a van and taken to Oakalla regional prison in New Westminster. I knew this would be my home for the next three weeks and possibly much longer. Jon York, whom I was busted with, had been sentenced to six months, so I knew anything could be possible.

As I arrived at the gate and was walked to the entrance of the jail, I saw people coming out that I knew. As one of them passed me he said, "Tell them, when you are being booked, that you are using and you want to go on the methadone program." I was terrified of what lay ahead of me. When it came time for me to be booked, sure enough they asked me if I was using and I said yes and I want to go on the methadone program. I had no idea what I was asking for, but would find out soon enough. Next I was asked to take off all my clothes, and I remember walking naked down a hall and being told to take a shower – something to do with lice, not too sure what. I was just very scared. Then of course another cavity search, after which I was handed my jail clothing and told to get dressed. I was escorted to my cell. I was only there a short while before someone came along and asked me to hold out my arm between the bars. I was told I was getting my injection of methadone. I had never taken methadone before nor was I addicted to any drugs. The next thing that happened was me nodding out on my bed. I know I experienced a lot more while I was being held but it is difficult for me to remember, as I was stoned the entire time I was in custody. At one point I was interviewed by a probation officer for my pre-sentence report. I remember it because I was so relieved he did not ask me about the methadone program I was on. He told me he was going to recommend a suspended sentence and that I would not do any more jail time.

I did come away from my jail experience with one good thing, though. Whenever I was out in the yard to get fresh air I would smoke a cigarette and then flick the butt. I would then watch two inmates fight over it. Right there and then I decided never to smoke again and I have never smoked a cigarette since.

I also learned about drag queens and realized that my stereotyping was wrong. It was the drag queens that protected me from the other crazies. The thing that shocked me the most was that there appeared to be just as many drugs inside the prison as there were outside on the street. These three weeks would haunt me for the rest of my life.

My custody was finished and I now knew what it was like to be wired. I stood up in front of the judge and was told I would be fined $500 and given an eighteen-month suspended sentence. I was very relieved not to be going back to jail. My father paid the fine and I was released.

I went immediately to see Julie, though I would only be with her a short while, as she was being sent to Italy for six months. What was uppermost in my mind was where I could score. I was wired. So off I went to find my brother.

JUNE 2, 3, 1967

THE FAMILY DOGS AND NW CO., WILLIAM TELL & THE MARKSMEN

I found this poster as a printing negative in my father's shop in 1985 while we were cleaning up after Dad passed away. I'd never seen this one before. I would still wait several years before printing it. Bob now has it on his website coloured one way, while Julie restored it coloured a different way. I do not remember putting on this event, as I could no longer get a

Poster 62
(The poster that never was) ➤

business licence once I had a criminal record. Whoever else did it without me, I do not know. After I closed the Afterthought events were put on without my knowledge!

On May 15 I turned 19. My reflection on my life to date was a little overwhelming and I knew my experience was quite different from my peers'. I had gone into jail a pothead and come out a junkie. Not quite what I had in mind. It was more than difficult. I was in denial that I had any kind of dependence on drugs. Up until now I had regularly watched Terry and his friends get high. Of course they all would insist they could take it or leave it, and that they just liked the rush when they injected themselves with heroin. Now I have my brother teaching me how to inject myself, commonly known as mainlining. It was easy to tell myself I did not have an addiction. I just wanted to get high all the time like most of Terry's friends. It is said that cannabis use leads to heroin use, but the only commonality is that both are illegal. How ironic that the place where I found out about addiction was behind bars in a provincial jail. It does seem kind of strange, as they also say there are no drugs in jail.

More than ten years later I would be working as a probation interviewer, and occasionally when the probation officers were overworked I would be asked to do a pre-sentence report. Whenever I would do one, I believe I would not have overlooked telling the judge whether the individual was on a methadone program. It seems this fact would have something to do with sentencing. As I have said repeatedly, the system is broken and it appears to me that no one is fixing it. I would continue my drug roller coaster ride for some time to come, and it would not be the system that would help me make the changes in my life to get me off that roller coaster. Instead, it was my faith and my soulmate that would make it possible for me to survive it all.

Thirty years later, while working as a correctional officer in Wilkinson Road jail on Vancouver Island, I would find out there are many things besides drugs in our jails. I would be held hostage at gunpoint. The management were quick to say that a gun had been smuggled in and that this was not the norm. I am sure that getting wired in jail was also not the norm. One of my fellow officers was shot in the arm while we were being held hostage. The inmate that had the weapon smuggled in was a convicted contract killer awaiting trial. I believe it was never his intention to escape but he wanted to improve conditions in the jail. The night before the hostage incident I was going through files of inmates who the staff believed might have the gun hidden. In looking at the files I was pretty sure one of these inmates had been a friend of my brother's. And it was this inmate who was now holding us hostage. I feel that his knowing my brother was a contributing factor in my being the first hostage to be released. He first asked me to switch the phone on in the office in order to start his negotiations and put forth his demands. Once that was done he told me I was not part of this and to get my little blank ass out of there. I did not make this statement at the time of my debriefing, as I didn't think anyone would have believed me. But I am sure the reason he released me was that he had known my brother from the street. It was many hours later that the other hostages were released.

JULY 1–8, 1967: TEENAGE FAIR

GROUP OF NINE POSTERS

Harry Ornest had decided to remove the Teenage Fair from the PNE, where it had been a fair within the larger fair, and make it a free-standing event. Over the years that the Teenage Fair was part of the larger exhibition, the PNE had wanted a bigger piece of the pie each year and Harry was tired of it. It seems that this greed scenario between corporations would continue to play out to this day. Wouldn't it be nice if people could be more content with what they have rather than always just wanting more?

So this Teen Fair would be at the Armouries in Kitsilano. It was a very large building, which made it possible for everything to be held indoors without worrying about weather. The place was large enough to house three stages, where the bands could play all at once. Harry had booked an incredible lineup from both the US and Canada. Since I had all my new-found experience with posters from my dance hall, I thought it would be cool if we could design a poster to feature each band.

It seemed that Bob Masse had decided to go south, as there were no more Afterthoughts, so I approached Frank Lewis to design these new posters. Frank had just put together a group of artists called the Hydrogen People and said they could create all the posters we required. [See "Hydrogen Sales" at page 211 in the Afterwords section.] As you look at these nine, you can tell they are strongly influenced by Frank's art style. I believe these were the start of creating posters for individual bands rather than particular events. Since I knew Afterthought posters had been collected by my customers, I thought why not sell posters? I worked out a split of the proceeds that made everyone happy.

After all, I now had a drug habit and I needed all the money I could get. In spite of the fact that I was stoned for most of the fair, it was somewhat successful.

Harry asked me if I would be interested in doing a fair in Toronto. Many years later I asked Julie if she knew why I had said no to Harry's offer. She simply said, "You were probably too stoned to say yes." Sad to say, she is probably right. Drugs can do strange things to your thinking! In any case, Harry was a terrific person and a wonderful mentor. I found it amazing how he stood by me. Sadly, Harry passed away several years ago – from natural causes, unlike some of my other friends. I am just sorry I never got to tell Harry how much he meant to me.

I am now footloose, so what to do? It seems a lot of people were going back east. My brother continued to introduce me to his many strange friends. One in particular, who had recently arrived from the east, had just started a franchise auto repair service and it seemed that he had more money than brains. My brother, true to form, introduced this friend to his favourite drug. It seems like Terry was the pied piper of heroin. It was very sad, but something my brother did not seem to see was that what he was doing was wrong. I was not surprised when this drug eventually led to his taking his own life from an overdose. Meanwhile, my brother's new-found friend and I spent a lot of time getting high with some of Terry's other friends. Then Terry announced he was going to hitchhike back east. This would not be the first time he had done this.

So, my soulmate was in Italy and my brother had left town. I remember visiting a friend's apartment where they were busy cutting up kilos of cannabis. Even though I was on probation I thought nothing of being there. At some point I imagined I had to tell somebody something important. I don't remember just what it was, but I decided to run out onto the balcony to tell them. Only problem was, the glass patio door was closed. And it did not stop me as I ran through the living room and right through the glass door, finally stopped by the balcony railing. It was a miracle I didn't go over. I did go to the emergency ward for stitches in my head. I still have the scar. My wife tells me she knew over in Italy that something had happened to me; she just didn't know what. After all of this I felt it was time for another road trip, so I filled the Mustang with people and set off for Toronto!

Poster 63 ➤

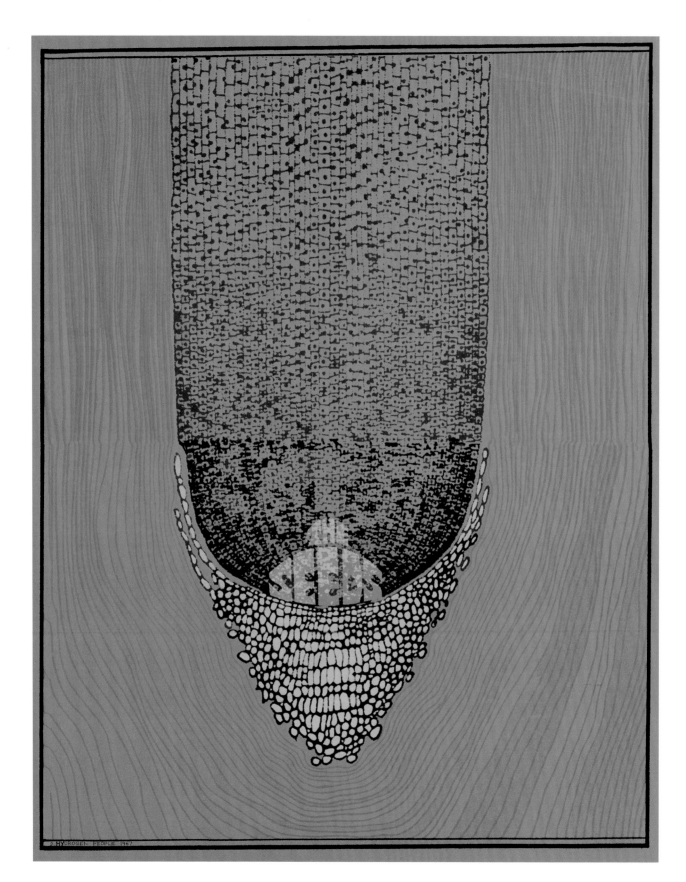

Poster 67 ➤

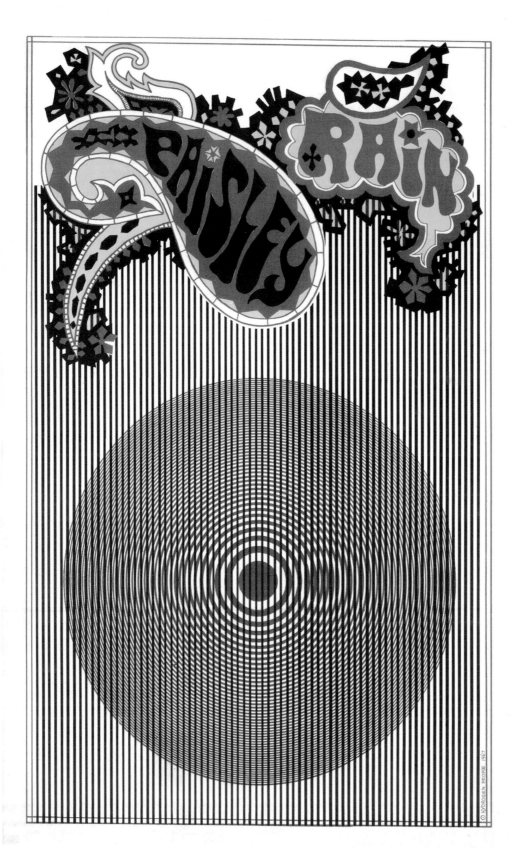

◄ *Poster 68*

▲ *Poster 71*

AUGUST 18, 1967: KITS THEATRE

UNITED EMPIRE LOYALISTS AND SEEDS OF TIME

Yes this is an Afterthought dance poster, and if you go back and look at poster 38 (opposite page 92) you will find its mate. The only differences are the colour, the date and one of the bands. I talked with Jeff and Anton from the United Empire Loyalists and Rocket from the Seeds of Time and no one can remember who put on this event. I know it was not me, because not only was I in Montreal at the time, I was also unable to put on any shows in Vancouver because I could not get a business licence, due to my recent conviction. It is troublesome because I still had Afterthought Enterprises, the company I had formed and was the only shareholder of. I suspect it was Roger Schiffer, my ex-partner, testing the waters, for shortly afterwards he opened the Retinal Circus.

My time in eastern Canada was crazy to say the least. In Toronto we crashed at a house run by the Company of Young Canadians, a group of young people funded by the federal government to do volunteer work. When I arrived in Toronto I was quite strung out. I then ran into an old folksinger friend who had taken a blank scrip pad from the office of his physician father. He told me he had this great idea that he would write scrip for Dexedrine and I would be the patient who would go into the drugstore to have the "prescription" filled. It would not be long before we had accumulated a lot of Dexedrine and had quite a business going. I look a lot younger than I actually am, which years later gave me the answer as to why it was so easy to get that scrip accepted at assorted pharmacies. Of course, it would not be long before I was strung out on speed.

Now my brother shows up and tells me he wants me to go to Montreal with him. We have a place to stay and Expo '67 is on. Of course I say yes and leave my good friends behind in Toronto with no way to get back to Vancouver. Not so good for my good friends, but I leave anyway. As we are driving to Montreal Terry asks me if I remember the sisters that stayed at his place in Vancouver. I say yes, and he says cool because that's where we are going to stay. We knock on the door of the address we have been given and this older man answers the door. We ask for the girls and are invited in. It turns out the girls are still living at home. We get treated like family and it was quite awesome, but I am

Poster 72 ➤

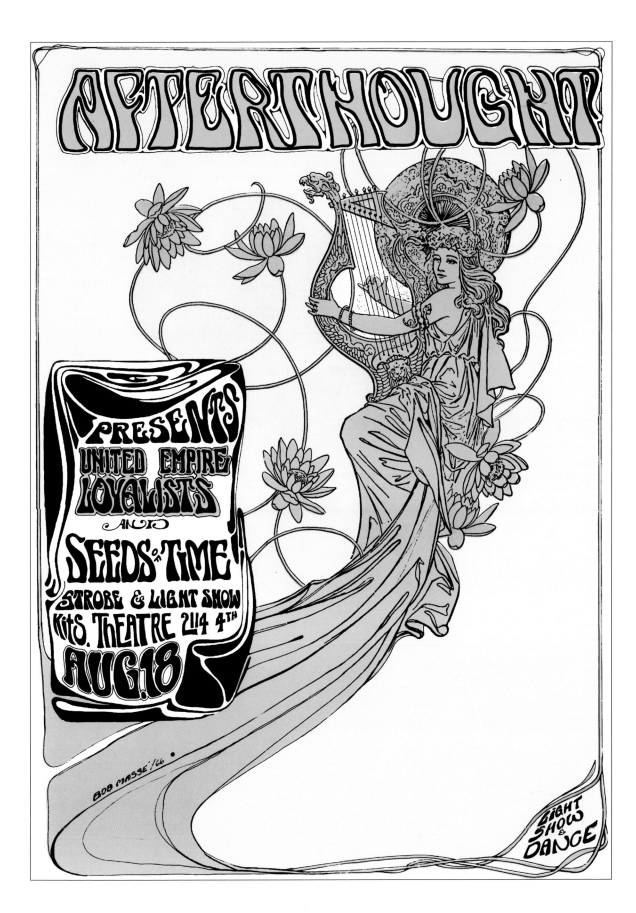

missing my soulmate, who is still in Italy. Somehow I find out she is flying back through Montreal. I spent an entire day at the airport, but it turned out her flight got changed and she had returned directly to Vancouver.

I tell Terry I am going back home because I miss Julie. Of course, he says that's cool. He just wants me to pick up a package at the post office from Teddy, our wealthy friend with the auto repair franchise. Apparently Teddy had returned to his home in Ontario to get himself straight, as he had been pretty strung out in Vancouver. The package at the post office, of course, was a bundle of heroin which he'd sent out before he left Vancouver just in case he needed it. We were all nervous about going into the post office, which is why they sent me. So what if I was on probation. And did I mention I had neglected to tell my officer I had left town, which broke a condition of my probation? I still cannot believe the stupid things I did back then and I am sure

none of my eight grandchildren would believe it. Both as a parent and grandfather I am now very anti-drugs, though I know that may be hard to believe given my background.

So now it is me, my brother and our friend driving non-stop to Vancouver, shooting up heroin all the way and taking speed as well, a very deadly combination. I would nod out while driving, and today I feel very fortunate to be alive to tell this story. Anyone who is young and reading this should be aware that drugs are dangerous and mixing drugs is even more dangerous. It is like playing Russian roulette. That said, I also feel that making drugs illegal does not prevent kids from doing them. That just feeds organized crime, and there has to be a better way.

Anyway, I did make it back alive and was thrilled to be reunited with Julie after this long separation. It just made my love for her stronger and I was thrilled to know she felt the same way. It is wonderful how strong love can be.

OCTOBER 27, 28, 1967: RETINAL CIRCUS

PH PHACTOR JUG BAND, PAINTED SHIP AND SEEDS OF TIME

So I am back from Toronto and Montreal and the only good thing about being back is getting to see Julie again. Our six-month separation has only affirmed how much I love her. There are a few problems, however. I am strung out but can't tell Julie or anybody else that I now have a serious drug habit.

The poster you'll see overleaf was given to me by my former partner, Roger Schiffer. It seems that while I was out of town he was able to establish a new dance hall with new partners. I found it interesting how much it resembled the Afterthought. This was quite understandable, as Roger had also been able to recruit my old light show, now renamed. He'd recruited Bob Masse too, although Bob only did one poster for him before leaving town. Roger managed to find a new artist, though: Eric Fisher of Magic Theatre Ltd. As Eric's work resembled Bob's so much, some of his posters got accredited to Bob. It was Bob who pointed this out to me; he had already left when Eric did these, including this one. The bands that had got their start at the Afterthought were more than happy to have a new venue to perform in. So it

would appear everyone was glad the dance hall business was again as it had been before, except I was no longer operating one. It is amazing how fast one can crash and burn.

I knew I could not dwell on the past and that I had to move ahead. But as I say, there were a few problems. First, I was strung out. Second, what I wanted to do I could not do, as I could not now get a business licence. But my biggest problem was that I had been busted again, this time for two joints. It seems I was being followed pretty much ever since I returned to Vancouver. The irony is that I was smoking whenever I could so I would not use other strange drugs. I knew enough not to carry drugs. At the time of the bust the joints were on the ground by Julie's car, which I was driving. Either way it didn't matter, I was charged one more time for possession. I was taken into custody, same search, into a holding cell and out on bail the next day. It would appear I was learning all too well how the system worked.

So I did the only thing I knew how to do: go back into the printing business. As mentioned earlier, my relationship with

my dad was somewhat rocky at the best of times. But I knew he was my father and doing the best he could, as he had his own personal problems. My parents had split up when I was quite young, so I really had no idea of what a normal family life was like.

I finally got off the insane drug roller coaster and after a long struggle was able to get myself together. I vowed to myself that my children would have a normal, stable childhood. I am still not certain

◄ *Poster 73*

how stable it was, but I know that Julie and I did the best we could. I am very proud of our children, as they have all grown up healthy, are married, have children of their own and are doing fine. None of them ever had to see the inside of a jail.

Right after our daughter Celeste was born my father too got it together. Unfortunately, my mother told me it was too late by then for her to forgive him.

Through the fall of 1967, difficult as it was, I worked for my father and when that did not pan out, I worked at other print shops.

FEBRUARY 3 AND 17, 1968: KALEIDOSCOPE AT GIBSON'S LANDING

PAISLEY RAIN

PAINTED SHIP

What do you do if you feel you are in a state of desperation. You are 19 years old and you have run a successful dance hall business that put on well over sixty events. Everyone seems to have a different story of the Afterthought and now everyone is going to the Retinal Circus. They are not aware of what happened, nor should they

care. For the patrons it was just a little pause in their summer, the Retinal Circus starting where the Afterthought left off. All is good for them; they have a place to go. The only problem is, I cannot be involved anymore. I am not allowed to have a business licence. I am on probation, which I have breached, and I am awaiting trial on

the kaleidoscope will present

THE
PAISLEY
RAIN

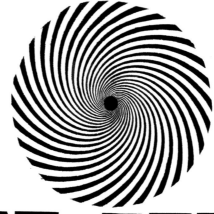

SAT. FEB.3
DANCE

AT

ROBERTS
CREEK
HALL

a new charge of possession of two joints of cannabis. Plus, I am still strung out from the habit acquired from my three-week stay in jail the first time around. What am I going to do?

As mentioned, I spent the latter half of 1967 working for my dad as a printer. I was not too happy doing this. The start of 1968 saw me working at a shoe warehouse. This was short-lived, however, and I still have the scar on my arm from a fight with another employee who used a steel pipe to make his point.

So what am I to do? I know I love promoting dances. It was the one thing I was successful at. I had basically no formal education, but I felt that promoting was in my blood. Now I was not allowed to do it anymore, so I needed to find a place where I could. In Vancouver in 1967 and '68 there were hippies who were moving to a place called Sechelt, to the small town of Gibson's Landing. The town would later become famous because of a TV series filmed there, *The Beachcombers*. My friends had been encouraging me to try to put on some dances. Gibson's was a remote place, so I should be able to get by without a licence. There was a small local hall on the outskirts so I thought why not?

The first event was on February 3, 1968. I'm sure you can tell I designed all of the posters and printed them myself at my father's shop. I had no money; I had lost it all. But I did have friends who had bands and were willing to help out. The first dance was okay but not a great attendance. I had not taken into account that there still were not a lot of people living in Gibson's. They would come later. So I attempted to do the best I could. I had a lot of setbacks, one being a BC Ferries strike which forced me to use a water taxi to transport everyone to Gibson's, a very expensive proposition. It just seemed that nothing was working out. I was raised on the west coast and this is the only time I can ever remember a ferry strike.

The only piece of equipment I had somehow been able to hang on to was a strobe light. I remember all too well the night of what would be my last event at Gibson's. The United Empire Loyalists were playing, the strobe light was going and everyone was dancing. All was good. Then I saw this very large man enter the hall. The strobe light made his movements seem slow motion. He ran to the stage and I watched in horror as he grabbed the strobe light in one large hand and crushed it with his other. All he had to do was tell me he did not like the strobe light. So the last piece of the Afterthought disappeared into memory. This event would be the end of my attempt to bring back a psychedelic dance hall.

◄ *Poster 74*

Poster 75 ▲

JULY AND AUGUST 1968: RIVERQUEEN, VANCOUVER

SONNY TERRY & BROWNIE MCGEE; DON CRAWFORD

Somehow I made it through the winter and into the spring of 1968, It was indeed a very difficult time. I continued to fight my drug addiction and still could not talk to anyone about it, including my soulmate. I do believe I was in total denial. I was

Poster 76 ➤

terrified of going back to jail and had no idea of what my future would bring. I had survived financially by doing whatever I had to do to get by.

The home furniture buyer for Woodward's department stores had opened a coffeehouse called the Riverqueen directly across from the Retinal Circus. He had modelled the place on the somewhat famous Riverboat coffeehouse located on Toronto's storied Yorkville Avenue, their equivalent of Vancouver's Fourth Avenue. In the summer of 1967 I had spent a lot of time on that Yorkville strip, cruising up and down in my Mustang. I thought it was so cool. The Riverboat just happened to be where I spent most of my time.

Julie had asked me to take her to the new Riverqueen, as Gordon Lightfoot was the act booked for its grand opening. The owner, whom I had met before, came up to me and asked me if I would like to manage his coffeehouse. He admitted he was losing money and had paid Lightfoot far too much. I thought it was a dream come true. I could not believe it. He knew what had happened to me but felt I could do a better job than he could. Of course I said yes and was overjoyed. As we watched Lightfoot I told Julie about my new job and that my start date was immediately. I have no memory of salary; I just was overwhelmed.

Now I had what I believed was a dream job. I had been given another chance. The first thing I was asked to do was book a big folk act. During my time running the Afterthought I was fortunate to have had the opportunity to talk with Albert Grossman, the famous music promoter from New York who handled the likes of Odetta, Peter, Paul & Mary, Ian & Sylvia, Bob Dylan and, yes, Gordon Lightfoot. I had no idea at the time, though, how important a promoter Grossman was.

Somehow (I don't remember exactly how) Albert had phoned me to see if I was interested in any of his groups. One I remember talking with him about was Sonny & Cher, who had a hit at the time with "I Want You, Babe." I decided against them because I didn't think you could dance to their music, but Albert did say to feel free to call him anytime.

I now needed a folk act, so I thought it would be a good opportunity to contact Albert. It was good to talk with him again and he suggested I book Sonny Terry & Brownie McGee. I remembered hearing them at the Bunkhouse coffeehouse and had thought they were fantastic. So of course I said yes. Now normally one would book an act like this for a week or two, but I had the opportunity to book them for three. I knew it was a risk but I took it. This was when I learned all the things you must do when you bring an established group to town. First you sign a contract and understand all its riders. Next, follow

Poster 77 ➤

through with everything in the contract. Sonny and Brownie's riders were very specific about what each of them required. They wanted to stay in different hotels; one wanted a kitchenette so he could prepare his own meals, while the other just needed a hotel room, as he liked to eat out. Of course, I also had to supply transportation to and from their hotels. I was more than willing to do everything they wanted, for I knew I was dealing with a legendary act. One thing I thought was peculiar, though, was that I had to make sure there was always a bottle of scotch and a bottle of milk backstage. It seems this was the must-have drink for Brownie McGee. Such was my introduction to scotch and milk.

The three weeks went by very quickly. The event was a great success and very profitable. What was more important to me was I also made two good friends.

It would be about ten years before I would see Sonny and Brownie again. I was now married to Julie, we had our first two children and I was working for the provincial government. At the time, I thought I was trying to save the world. The Kiwanis service club had brought Sonny and Brownie to the Comox Valley as a fundraiser. I was ecstatic to see them again. I could not help but think how fortunate I was to have gotten to where I was at this time. I was quick to invite them to our house for dinner. However, I had forgotten that the two of them still did nothing together except their act onstage. So it would be only Brownie that would be our dinner guest and who would meet our children. Brownie invited all of us to come visit him in LA. Unfortunately that never happened, for by the time we were able to do so, he had passed away. They were wonderful people, both of them, and I was fortunate to have them as friends. I learned a lot from them and still miss them.

The next Riverqueen act was from Toronto: Don Crawford. He had played for me at the Afterthought when he was experimenting with being a folk rock act. That hadn't worked out for him, so he'd returned to his roots. I booked him for the standard week, as this was just your typical coffeehouse date. But I must say that Don put on a good show.

For reasons I'm not sure of – but I believe was because of debt from the club's high opening expenses – the Riverqueen was struggling. So when Gary Taylor – formerly the drummer with one of Les Vogt's bands, the Classics, and now a club owner himself – offered to buy the place and turn it into a jazz room, the owner jumped at the offer and that was the end of a great job for me. [See Related Reading at "Bill Aicher" for an article on Gary Taylor.]

AUGUST 31 TO SEPTEMBER 3, 1968:

SKY RIVER ROCK FESTIVAL & LIGHTER-THAN-AIR FAIR, SULTAN, WASHINGTON

NUMEROUS BANDS, INCLUDING THE GRATEFUL DEAD

I am now am getting really depressed. I have lost my job running the Riverqueen coffeehouse, as it was sold and became Gary Taylor's Show Lounge. My friends are telling me about a great rock festival to be held in the Pacific Northwest, a first of its kind. Every band you could think of is appearing. Julie wants to go, as does another couple, Ron Ulmer and Joanne Rocco. Ron had worked on the light show at the Afterthought. So I thought why not.

We all piled into my car and headed off to the festival. When we arrived the place was a sea of people. It was incredible. I had never seen anything like it before. This was the start of rock festivals in the Northwest and there would be many more to come. The event that would attract the most attention nationally would be Woodstock in New York, of course, which was a year after Sky River. Nevertheless, this festival was incredible. Unfortunately I do not have any memories of it. Julie tells me that this is because I was too stoned, and I am sure she is right. She tells me that not long after

we got there, she slipped into a mudhole and got soaking wet and dirty. As she did not have a change of clothing, I drove her home to get changed (a three-hour trip, by the way). Fortunately for us, her parents were away in Italy, so we spent the night at their house and then returned to the festival. When we found Ron and Joanne, they did not even know we had been gone.

We spend the day grooving to the music and of course I get more stoned. We met up with a lot of old friends from both sides of the border. Dusk was approaching and Julie tells me she does not want to sleep on the ground, so we round up Ron and Joanne and head off to find a place to stay. Seattle was the closest, but this posed more of a problem than we first thought, because our funds were very limited. After driving around – and I do mean driving around – we find a room in an old house for $90 a night. We have the top floor and there are two separate rooms with beds that pull out of the wall. The next morning we return for day three of the festival and

of course have one more day of fantastic music. As the festival starts to wind down the Grateful Dead appear on stage. They had not been booked but had heard about what was going on and drove up from San Francisco to perform.

We are ready to leave but we cannot find Ron. It turns out he was in the medical tent.

◄ *Poster 78*

He had forgotten to take out his contacts the night before and his eyes had swollen shut. So it's just the three of us returning from the festival. As we are leaving, Julie sees this poster on a telephone pole, so of course she takes it to add to her now fairly large collection. Ron would return to Vancouver a few days later and is alive and well to this day, as is Joanne. The four of us we are still friends after all these years.

OCTOBER 31 TO NOVEMBER 3, 1968: RETINAL CIRCUS

VELVET UNDERGROUND AND BLACK SNAKE BLUES BAND

It seems appropriate that this should be the last poster of the sixties that I have a story for. It is my understanding that this was also Roger Schiffer's last Retinal Circus poster. I find it interesting that the first poster I commissioned was done by Frank Lewis and that Frank would be the artist to create Roger's last one. I'm happy to say that I had spoken with Frank just as he turned 80. I'd phoned him to wish him happy birthday and we had a good talk about the old times. This would also be the last poster I would give Julie. Yes, I know it's a handbill and not a poster. Roger and I never could agree on which was better.

I am now in court again, facing my fate. The judge finds me guilty of breach of probation and possession of two joints of cannabis. I am sentenced to eighteen months jail. This hits me like a sledge-hammer. I am taken into custody and again back to the holding cells. I am re-membering that the last time I was on my way to jail I went in as a pothead and came out a junkie. This time around, when they ask me if I have a drug prob-lem I tell them no. I think to myself that I don't want their help to get straight. I would rather do it on my own.

I was first sent back to Oakalla, where I waited to find out where I would do my time and how much time it would be. It was not pleasant to reflect back to the first time I was in these same cells. Finally I was told I would be sent to the Haney Correctional Institution, which I was told was a newish institution for young offenders aged 18 to 30 located about 30 miles from Vancouver. This distance would become an issue for Julie, as she would come to visit me every week. I tried to get transferred to a camp closer to Vancouver but was told I posed a flight risk, as the place was minimum security.

A short time after my arrival in Haney I was assigned to Pine Ridge Camp, a minimum security facility on the grounds of the institution. It did seem strange that I would be put in a minimum security camp after all, when before I couldn't go to the one closer to Vancouver because it was minimum security. But why wouldn't it be confusing?

I am now in an institution where I have no control of my time, but I feel blessed that I am not behind bars anymore. Yet I still know I can't just walk away from this, that I must serve my sentence, however long it turns out to be.

I felt that the best use of my time at Pine Ridge was to go to school, given that I had so little education. The school was situated in the main part of Haney, so every weekday I would walk approximately a quarter of a mile to attend classes. On weekends I would attend chapel, receive family visits and work out with weights, trying to get as buff as I could. I needed to match my fellow inmates in order to survive.

Pine Ridge Camp consisted of what were called bunkhouses. In these buildings were 12 bunkbeds in a room with a woodstove in the middle for heat. All of your possessions were kept under or near your bunk and that was your daily life. An interesting side note is that my fellow bunk mates informed me that under the woodstove was a hiding place accessed by moving the woodstove. We would collect food scraps from the kitchen to make homebrew, which we'd store under the woodstove. I am not sure how people managed to do this but they did and never got caught. It certainly made me wonder about what I was in jail for.

I do not want to make it appear that my time at Pine Ridge was a cakewalk. It was very difficult. I arrived there as a scrawny kid trying to hold my own. When I was released I was fortunate to walk out with all my body parts and no tattoos, which I figured was a win that I had been able to survive this experience.

After being transferred to the camp I was finally able to see my soulmate, my lover Julie. The visiting conditions were far better than last time, when we had to talk separated by glass and using telephones. This time we sat at a table in the

Poster 79 ➤

same room with guards watching us. Julie would continue to visit me while I was in custody. We had no idea at the time how long I would remain in the camp. It was on one of the early visits that I found out Julie was pregnant with our child. At first this was hard to grasp, that I was going to be a father. But it was much harder for Julie, as she had no one to go to. Her family did not know she was pregnant or that I was in jail.

Christmas was rapidly approaching and I could not comprehend not having a family Christmas. I was quite aware that my family was somewhat dysfunctional, but nevertheless they were my family.

My love was pregnant with our child and I didn't know what to do. Earlier I had been introduced to the chaplains and they were the only ones of the staff I felt I could talk to. I found out there was a chance I could get out on a Christmas pass. Unfortunately that did not happen, because I was still considered to be a flight risk and to have not yet understood the seriousness of my offence. I must admit I did not understand then nor have I ever understood the seriousness of my offence.

I was only able to survive through Christmas because of my love for Julie and knowing and believing I would eventually get out. My faith too enabled me to believe I could get through this. The last thing was music, because it helped me heal. Julie was able to bring me her turntable along with the Beatles' *White Album*. All these things made it possible for me to survive through it all. That Christmas would be the first and last one I would spend without family. To this day, holidays are a difficult time for me. It would be many years before I would be in a jail again, except by then it would be because of my job, as I would end up working for the Attorney General of BC. Strange how things work out.

The one thing that helped me when I was in jail as an inmate was the chaplaincy program. The chaplain was always there for me. He helped me with my faith and to get through my hard times. Recently I visited a local correctional facility in my role as a member of the Downtown Victoria Churches Association. I have been part of this organization for over twenty-four years. It is something I'm pleased about in that it is so important for all faiths to work together. While visiting the jail the chaplain reported on a music program they had put together. I thought of how many times the chaplaincy program had been threatened or in some cases suspended, but somehow it continues to do its good work.

It does seem strange as I write this chapter of my life that possession of cannabis is now legal in two US states, yet our Conservative government is stronger than ever in their war on drugs. One wonders if they will ever learn. I do believe there is hope for the next generation of politicians to correct these wrongs.

I continued to do my time with a whole lot of unbelievable events taking place. For anyone who questions whether there is abuse of all types in jail, I know from first-hand experience that there is. And yes there are all the same drugs available on the inside as there are on the street. From the time I was sentenced I would try to get out. Even though I knew I could just walk away, I also knew that in time I would get caught. They had me trained like some kind of dog. Every time I would ask my discharge date, it would change. It was early spring and I was told I would have a chance at early parole because I had now done six months, or one-third of my eighteen-month sentence. My parole hearing came up and I was turned down. I was then told I would have to go back to court, as I was in breach of my probation when I was arrested the second time.

I appeared in court and was told that because of the breach of probation I would be doing an additional nine months, which was how long I had left on my probation. Where I had to break this news to Julie was right in the courtroom as I was sentenced to this additional time. She was not happy, to say the least. It was early April and our baby was due in June. Julie remembers very well going to her father crying and telling him what had happened. Her father then phoned his sister, our Aunt Rina, to ask if she could do anything to help. It seems she knew the right people, for I was out on national parole the next day. Julie and I were married May 10, 1969, and have now been happily together for forty-five years. We must be doing something right.

AFTER THE AFTERTHOUGHT

THE NEXT YEARS

I am out of jail and the first thing to do is get married. We set the date and find an apartment. We move to New Westminster on the advice of my parole officer, who said it would be best if we did not live in the Vancouver area, so I could resist any temptations that arose. However, the parole officer did not know my brother, who greeted my release by asking me if I wanted to get high. It just seemed natural to say yes.

Our daughter Celeste was born in July of that year and was greeted by all with joy. She was the first grandchild on both sides of the family and was immediately spoiled by all of her grandparents. The biggest surprise was my father, who immediately became a true grandfather to Celeste. By the time our other children arrived he had stopped drinking and smoking and was a model grandfather, visiting us often and spoiling the children whenever he could get the chance. It is amazing the power of grandchildren. I am grateful that I stayed friends with my father until he passed away, and that our children have wonderful memories of him.

My father-in-law was good enough to give me a job with his company building and repairing sawmills. My task was that of a helper, driving truck, picking up materials etc. It was my first blue-collar job. I am very grateful for what my father in-law did for me, as he gave me a chance when no one else would. The one big problem is I came out of jail with more baggage than I went in with, and the only way I believed I could cope was to get high. This job lasted about a year and by then I believed I could make it on my own by establishing a marketing and printing business with Frank Lewis as my partner (without a licence of course). I called it Celestial Press, after our daughter. As I look back I am amazed that my parole officer never questioned anything. Whoever he was, he had a lot to learn.

At this time I would never dream I would end up in the same line of work. This business, I now know, was a front and an excuse to get high more often. I was getting

wired again and of course was in complete denial about it. After being out of jail just over a year I was out one evening when my wife found me downtown attempting to crank up. I was all by myself at the time. It was very scary. I attempted to rationalize what I was doing but I knew I had a problem. Julie simply said, "You stop now or you lose me and your daughter." It was that simple. I had a choice and I made it. I did not get high that night nor have I ever cranked up again. This was the end of my roller coaster ride The next time I would be sticking a needle in my arm was when I needed to inject myself with interferon so I could beat hepatitis C. Julie had warned me there would be a price to pay for what I had done to myself. I'm very proud to say that I am now drug-free, without any dependence.

I started to get involved at the beginning of the Gastown scene in Vancouver, but it did not take long for me to figure out that if I continued in that milieu, it would take me to places I did not want go.

So what am I going to do? I knew what I liked to do, which was to promote events. And I knew I was good at it, so I could promote and stay out of trouble. I decided to get my Grade 12 first. I did this at night school. I then learned of a two-year program to become a financial assistance worker, helping social workers deliver

Poster 80 (Hippie Daze) ➤

services to clients. I had figured out that what I really wanted was a social work or law degree, but I knew that could not happen. Still, I was confident that by working on the side and with student loans I could complete the course. But first I had to get accepted into the program.

It was difficult, but ironically what helped a lot was exactly my background in promoting. Shortly after I started at Vancouver City College I was asked if I would like to be their activity coordinator. I asked what was involved and they said putting on concerts. I said great, how much does it pay? They said it doesn't pay, it's volunteer. So my first task was to make it a paying job, which I did. Next I was to put on a concert and I had no troubles, as I still had all my old contacts. When I phoned booking agent and manager Sam Feldman, he was more than willing to help and suggested I book jazz master Paul Horn. I did and the concert was a great success. It felt good to be back in the business again. After graduating from college I moved our family to Vancouver Island and went to work for the provincial government.

I then had an opportunity to run an alternative sentencing initiative called the Community Work Service program, or cws. It gave young offenders the opportunity to do meaningful work in the community, as opposed to going to jail. What a concept! I only wish I would have had that kind of chance in my youth. I operated this program in the Comox Valley.

One day I received a phone call from Tom Northcott, who was now married and had children and was working as a commercial fisherman. I was glad to hear from him, as we had lost touch over the years. Tom told me he was having a problem with his teenage son, who apparently had been busted for possession of cannabis. Tom wanted to know if I could help, as he did not want his son to go to jail. I said I would be glad to help and would see what I could do. I spoke with the prosecutor and he agreed that cws would be in order. Tom's son was then ordered to cws with a suspended sentence, which meant he would have no criminal record. I was glad to help, and again, it's strange how things work out. Tom would eventually go back to school and become a lawyer. Many years later I would be putting on a benefit for an alternative high school program, and when I asked if he would perform he said, "Of course," without the slightest hesitation.

JULY 1975: COMOX VALLEY RENAISSANCE FAIR

It was now almost ten years since the Afterthought was born. I was still happily married to Julie and we now had two children: Celeste, now 6, and Damian, 2. Everything seemed perfect. I had now been working for the provincial government for two years as a financial assistance worker with a territory from Union Bay to the Comox Valley that included Denman and Hornby islands. It was for me at the time a perfect job. I was able to help people who were on social assistance to get back to being productive members of society. Unfortunately, not knowing any better at the time, I did everything I could to keep my past a secret. I was embarrassed about the fact that I was an ex-junkie and an ex-con. The thought of someone finding out was terrifying to me, so I talked very little about my promoting years. As I reflect back, I see how much easier life could have been if only I had been more truthful about my past. It would take a long time – until all our children were grown – that I would learn that "only the truth can set you free." Many friends would come to visit us from Vancouver and farther away. Some came and stayed. My closest friend, Wayne G., still lives in the valley along with his wife and grown son. So in time

it became known that I had been a music promoter, even though I had done everything I could to keep it quiet.

So it was not a surprise when I was asked to be on the board of the Renaissance Fair. Several locals and some of the new people who had moved into the valley felt the place needed an annual music festival, and thus the idea of the Fair was born. It became a regular event that continued for eight years. The poster you see overleaf was, as its headline says, for the last one. The event would later be reborn as the Courtenay Music Festival, operated by a well-known musician and promoter named Doug Cox. This festival has become well regarded throughout Canada.

I'm proud to look back now and know I played a small part in the Renaissance Fair. The problem was that it took so long for me to get over being afraid of my past. At the time, I was convinced that every needless death of a young person that occurred in the sixties was somehow my fault. It was a large burden I carried for many years. I still do not know why there were then and still continue to be so many young people that take their own life when there is so much to live for. A lot of the deaths in the sixties and later were good friends, and

THE LAST
COMOX VALLEY
RENAISSANCE FAIR

JULY 6,7,8

11:00 am — 11:00 pm
$5.00 per day
Children under 12 & Seniors free

WESTCOAST SHOWCASE OF CRAFTS

with music, children's theatre & international food & featuring mimes,
clowns, storytellers, wandering minstrels & visual arts

ONE MILE NORTH OF COURTENAY ON HEADQUARTERS ROAD — FOLLOW SIGNS
(No Blanket Booths — No Drugs — No Dogs

OUR PARENT BODY FUNDED BY
MINISTRY OF PROVINCIAL SECRETARY & GOVERNMENT
SERVICES, CULTURAL SERVICES BRANCH, VICTORIA, B.C.

Printed in Canada, March 1984

INFORMATION 338-6211
367 - 4th ST.
COURTENAY, B.C. V9N 1G8

include my own brother. I wish other families' relatives alive today would not blame the past for what occurred.

I now know a lot of good came out of the sixties as well, much more positive than negative. In the end everyone is responsible for their own actions.

◀ *Poster 81*

NEW YEAR'S, CA. 1983: CFB COMOX

LYNN BROOKS & HOMEGROWN

Lynn Brooks was a dear friend who I thought of as my big sister. In the sixties she would attempt to keep me out of trouble in those turbulent times.

In the early eighties, now fifteen years on from the birth of the Afterthought, Lynn phoned me from Seattle, her hometown. She'd moved back there from Vancouver just before we'd moved to the Island. Lynn tells me she now has a great new group called Homegrown and she wants to come and visit us. All I need to do is find a gig to cover their expenses. I'm not sure how I did it, but I was able to get the band a gig at the Comox airbase to play for the Canadian Forces New Year's bash. The event was a great success and it was hard for me not to want to get back into the business. When the entire band showed up at our house, you couldn't help but notice heads turning in the neighbourhood. The whole group was African American,

and at that time the Comox Valley was predominantly a WASP community. It was indeed a different lifestyle.

We now had three children – Celeste, Damian and Justine – and we felt our family was complete. I was working for the probation department of the provincial government, running a program intended to be an alternative sentencing program. I was thrilled to be able to offer youth an alternative to jail. By this time the government was starting to figure out that incarceration was not always the answer to positive change. Unfortunately the pendulum has now swung back again and our present Conservative government believes harsh incarceration works. As Bob Dylan would say, "the times they are a-changin'" and sometimes not for the better.

The years we were able to stay and raise our children in the Comox Valley were great. While preparing this chapter,

▲ *[Figure 82b] (Lynn in Mexico 2009)*

▲ *[Figure 82a] (Lynn Brooks and Tom Shepard, Pender Street 1966)*

though, I learned that Frank Lewis, who I have always felt was my brother, had died from cancer. He too was one of those that came out to the Island to visit and never went back to the city. The Island was good to him. There are murals all over that he was responsible for. I can't help but remember the first poster he did for me and think about how the powers that be actually got upset because Frank drew flowers coming out of Tom Northcott's head (see poster 6 opposite page 14).

In the mid-eighties the government of the day, which was right-wing, decided in their wisdom to privatize the community service program I was running, and thus I was without a job. But talk about a full circle: the system found me a position in Victoria at the regional corrections centre. I would be back in jail!

FEBRUARY 21, 23, 1998: VICTORIA, BURNABY

PEARSON COLLEGE PRESENTS ONE WORLD

In 1985 I was transferred to Victoria, where I started yet another phase of my life. The government had asked me to work as a correctional officer. So here I am working in Wilkinson Road jail. I find it very hard to believe that 16 years earlier I was in jail on the other side of the bars. It did not take me long to realize there was very little difference other than I got to go home at the end of my shift.

I reflect back to my correctional service training at the Justice Institute. During the course I stayed at a hotel in Vancouver and went home for the weekends. It was during the week that Aunt Rina phoned and invited me over for dinner. I had just arrived back at the hotel and I remember telling her I was still in my uniform and needed to go change. She said don't bother, just come as you are. When I arrived for dinner I could tell Aunt Rina was so proud of me. I thought about what a horrific journey I had taken to get to this point in my life. It was Aunt Rina that strongly suggested that I apply for a pardon, as she was so proud that I had turned my life around. Of course, when I got back to Victoria I told Julie about the dinner. It felt strange to see the power of a uniform. Nevertheless I did apply and received an unconditional pardon. Now, as a grandfather, I look back and savour the fact that I have no criminal record.

It was shortly after my training that I was involved in a hostage incident at the jail. No one ever told me it would be possible for an inmate to have a gun smuggled into jail, but it happened. As a result of this incident I eventually quit my job as a civil servant and was diagnosed and treated for post-traumatic stress disorder.

The next ten years were again a roller coaster ride I did not anticipate. I tried to do many different things. One of my first volunteer activities was with the Intercultural Association (ICA). I found them in the phone book and thought it sounded interesting. One thing I have learned is that our world could be very much improved simply by racial understanding of each other. Bill McElroy, at that time the CEO of the association, helped me learn lot about cultural understanding. Bill remains a good friend.

During my time as a volunteer at ICA I heard about Veselka, a Ukrainian dance troupe based in Victoria and comprised of children and young adults. This made me reflect back to my preteens when I did Ukrainian dancing. It would be one of the few good memories from my youth. These memories prompted me to ask our children if they would like to try out Ukrainian dancing. They agreed and this led to another chapter in my life. I would become a member of Veselka's board of directors, then president of the society and business manager. I was able to help arrange some tours for the group and had some great family adventures with them. I had originally not written about this chapter of my life, as I thought it was more about our children. But I recently attended an original performance produced by Veselka where I watched my grandson Ethan dance. What a proud moment. I watched the fantastic show staged by Liza Hall, the creative director for Veselka, and reflected back to when I first met Liza as one of the dancers with my own kids. She has come a long way. Veselka has evolved into a great dance troupe, winning awards whenever they compete. I am proud to have played a small role in their success. Frank Lewis did a graphic for Veselka.

Just one more afterthought which came to me while watching Veselka's latest performance: all the kids from the troupe, who are now adults, are doing well. There's definitely something to be said about positive involvement for youth.

A lot happened on this journey of understanding, which led me in 1997 to Pearson College, one of nine "world colleges" in various countries that promote racial understanding. In time I would be offered an opportunity to manage a One World Concert, which is the poster pictured here. Of course, I knew you had to have a good poster to have a good event. This one was designed by the students. I pray we could

Poster 83 ➤

UNITED IN SORROW   UNITED IN JOY 1998

ONE WORLD

Pearson College presents an eclectic performance of **song & dance** by a cast of 200 students from **80 countries**

Saturday, February 21, 2 pm & 8 pm Royal Theatre, Victoria

VICTORIA TICKETS @ McPHERSON BOX OFFICE & OTHER TICKET OUTLETS 386-6121

Monday, February 23, 2 pm Michael J. Fox Theatre, Burnaby

VANCOUVER TICKETS CALL (604) 664-8560

do much more to promote understanding, for in the end we are all the same.

The highlight of my contract was a concert where Pearson College students backed up Eric Bibb, who is the son of folksinger and actor Leon Bibb. Leon is an old friend from the sixties. The performance took place on the Variety Club telethon, a fundraiser for children. The Barnett brothers had been instrumental in getting the telethon started, so it was easy for me to get the college onto the bill. Eric was doing a very moving song that was a tribute to Nelson Mandela. I later learned from Eric that he was able to perform the song for "Madiba" in person. I only wish I could have been there.

While the students were still in Vancouver I had them perform a concert at the Terry Fox Theatre. It was indeed a memorable time for all.

SPRING 1998

FARMER'S DAUGHTER

In the spring of 1998 I was asked by Bob Bryant to help promote Farmer's Daughter. They were an up-and-coming country group that could have, should have, made it to the big time. However, it was not to be. My time with Bob was a journey that evolved into a company called Northern Lights, a distributor of glow products. The enterprise would succeed in obtaining the glow distribution rights for the 1999 Pan American Games in Winnipeg, my hometown. Talk about a full circle. Our son, Damian, would end up working with Bob.

Poster 84 ➤

HEPATITIS C REHAB

VICTORIA LATIN FEST 2003

With the beginning of the new century would come the most changes in my life.

Ever since the prison hostage incident I had been aware that my life had changed. I

Sunshine Coast Country Music Festival

Nitty Gritty Dirt Band

Farmer's Daughter

Prairie Oyster

Susan Aglukark

Amy Sky

August 14, 15 & 16, 1998

★ *Artists' Autographs and Souvenirs* ★
★ *Food & Merchandise Concessions* ★
★ *Sunshine Saloon* ★
★ *Children's Tent* ★

ON-SITE CAMPING, RV AND AUTO PARKING NEXT TO THE FESTIVAL GROUNDS

Duane Steele

Patricia Conroy

Gary Fjellgaard

Featuring Over 20 Top Performers

TICKETS ON SALE NOW!

Monday – Friday 9:00am to 5:00pm

Sunshine Coast (604) 740-9993

Toll Free 1-888-984-9777

WEEKEND PASS $110.00
DAY PASS $45.00
TAXES INCLUDED

PLUS SPECIAL EVENT

Enjoy an intimate concert!

LORD JIM'S RESORT HOTEL V.I.P. BARBECUE

AUGUST 14, 15 & 16
5:00pm to 7:00pm Nightly

Valdy • Gary Fjellgaard • Sue Medley

$115.00 per person includes
DAY PASS + Transportation to/from Festival Grounds
Limited tickets available:

1-888-757-3474

PRESENTED BY

Suzanne Gitzi

Rick Tippe

Dick Damron

would always reflect on my past and wonder how I'd survived to this point. When I was being treated for post-traumatic stress disorder my psychologist told me this was normal for what had occurred. It was surreal and I thought about how it would affect my family.

The PTSD isn't my only health issue just now, either. I am also seeing specialists for a diagnosed hiatus hernia. I am told I need surgery. Meanwhile, Celeste and Damian, within a week of each other, announce their intention to get married. Both Julie and I are thrilled for both of them.

I did not know what the result of the surgery would be and of course was told there were no guarantees, so I postponed it until after the weddings. The operation took more than six hours and apparently proved more difficult than expected. When I came out of the fog, my doctor and friend Barry Gelling told me the surgery was a success. But the news was not all good: I had a healthy liver but I also had hepatitis C.

Hepatitis C explained the health difficulties I'd been having. I also found out that many close friends had it too. I would wait to seek treatment until I felt I had no choice. The treatment was interferon, which would be 48 weeks of injecting myself twice a week and taking daily medication as well. When I finally began the treatment, the irony of it was I would feel sicker each time I took an injection, even though it was making me better. If it was not for the love of my family and my faith in God I question whether I would have made it.

It became very difficult. Julie would often say to me, "Did you not think there would be a price to pay for your past?" A close friend, Aaron Gordon, convinced me I had to do something other than feel sorry for myself. He suggested I volunteer for VIRCS, the Victoria Immigrant & Refugee Centre Society). He felt I could help them with their Latin Festival. This volunteering would eventually lead to a full-time job promoting the festival.

After completing my treatment I would find out I was hep C free. The odds of beating it were very low. I felt very blessed and now I had the opportunity to work at what I was happiest doing, which is promoting music. Only this time it was Latin instead of rock and roll. I reflected back to when I had had a chance to book Carlos Santana back in the sixties. I had passed on him then because I thought Latin music would never make it. It took me thirty years to find out how fantastic this style is!

Poster 85 ➤

VICTORIA LATIN FEST 2004

I now had a couple of Latin Fests under my belt. They were successful by way of both revenue and the good time had by all. These were very different from past events I'd done. I had to learn that the main purpose of this festival was first to earn income to help operate VIRCS, which is a non-profit organization set up to help new Canadians and immigrants fit into our society, aiding them in learning English and finding employment.

The festival had been presented for a number of years prior to my coming on board, but it was a very difficult situation, as their the regular staff had very little experience in any type of event planning. It seemed like everyone was learning on the job. After the first year, Julie too would join VIRCS, as an employment counsellor, and she would also coordinate the children's activities for the festival.

I also looked for music business connections in Victoria. There was an agency called Atomique Productions, which had been active for a number of years in the city. Atomique was run by Gary Vanbusker, whom I had met in the '60s, when he was promoting in Victoria at the same time I was doing so in Vancouver. Gary introduced me to two up-and-coming promoters who were working with him: Nick Blasko and Dimitri Demers.

It was interesting to meet them, as they were schoolmates of our son Damian, and during their school days had hung out at our house.

After the first year that I was involved with the festival I approached Bob Masse to volunteer to do posters for it. It was a big change for him, as it was not rock, but these posters helped take the festival to another level. Each year, the festival improved, and I am grateful to Bob for agreeing to help.

In 2004 we expanded the Latin Festival's run from one week to two, but everything started to change in VIRCS after the death of my good friend Aaron Gordon. He had been the anchor of the board of directors and president of the society. It was a very unexpected death, of cancer. It was a difficult time for me, as it was Aaron who had got me out my depression by getting me to volunteer for VIRCS. Life takes some very strange turns: Aaron had helped me through a lot of difficult times and now I was attending his funeral. The Latin Fest continued for a few more years, but after Aaron's passing the life seemed to have gone out of it. I left after the 2004 event and it eventually disappeared into the history of Victoria.

Poster 86 ➤

APRIL 2005

SUNSHINE WHEELS BENEFIT

While I was being treated for hepatitis C I received a phone call from Peter Barnett asking me if I would like to be on the board of the Sunshine Wheels Foundation. The purpose of this non-profit would be to raise funds and awareness of the need for bicycles in developing countries. I was honoured to be asked and we did what we could to fulfill this mandate.

One of the fundraising ideas was to do a benefit concert with Country Joe. I had not talked with Joe since the sixties but when I phoned him it seemed like it had been just last week since we talked. I explained what I wanted and he agreed. We set dates for concerts in both Victoria and Vancouver. All of the band members were able to perform except for guitarist Barry ("The Fish") Melton. Again I phoned my friend Bob Masse, and he was quick to volunteer to do a poster.

The first show was in Vancouver and then over to Victoria. For the Victoria concert I had invited a lot of old friends who were now living on the island, including family. Joe started the show and throughout the concert he would tell stories the way he always did. But as mentioned earlier at page 131, when he told the story of me going to

jail for nine months for possession of cannabis I was as shocked as Julie was.

And of course, Joe also told his banana story, which, by the way, is also on his web site. And as an afterthought, so to speak, I realized that the way he told it was different from the way I remembered it. You see, on trips down to San Francisco we routinely stop at drummer Gary "Chicken" Hirsh's place, and on our last time down there I told Chicken about this book of posters and stories that was going to be published. When I related to him what I'd written about the banana story, he said it was close but not quite accurate. He told me the house I had gone to back then was in Vancouver, not Berkeley, and that he was the one that came up with the banana peel idea. I still believe it happened in Berkeley, but Chicken's version may also be true. Hey, it was the sixties, and as the old joke goes, "If you think you remember those days, you probably weren't there!"

Anyway, it was a lot of work to do both concerts and I had a lot of help from a lot of friends. Unfortunately the shows were not completely sold out and as a result were not a financial success. Still, these two good shows were enjoyed by all who came.

Poster 87 ➤

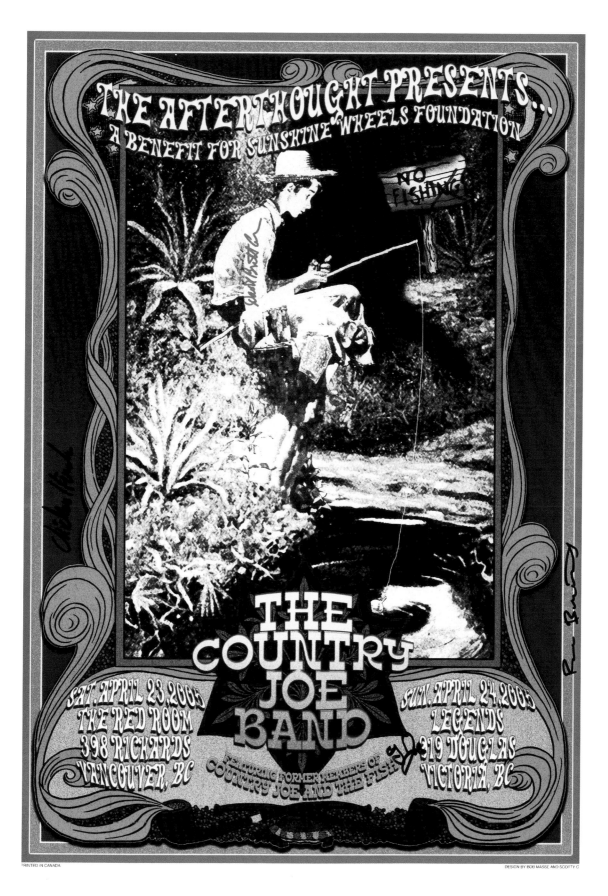

THE AFTERTHOUGHT PRESENTS...
A BENEFIT FOR SUNSHINE WHEELS FOUNDATION

NO FISHING

THE COUNTRY JOE BAND

SAT. APRIL 23, 2005
THE RED ROOM
398 RICHARDS
VANCOUVER, BC

FEATURING FORMER MEMBERS OF
COUNTRY JOE AND THE FISH

SUN. APRIL 24, 2005
LEGENDS
919 DOUGLAS
VICTORIA, BC

DESIGN BY BOB MASSE AND SCOTTY C

THE REST OF MY LIFE

GASTOWN POSTER

I chose this poster to bring my story up to the present time. Frank Lewis drew this one, and I as I write this second-last chapter I am grieving the loss of a very close friend. I had phoned Frank in December 2012, on his 80th birthday. We talked about his maybe creating a cover for this book. He said his health was not good, and as it turned out the cover was not to be. Frank had come to stay with us when we lived in the Comox Valley. I know he had a profound effect on all of our children. They referred to him as Uncle Frankie and all have fond memories of him. It was a good time in our family life.

As I finish this chapter I'm looking out over Lake Elsinore in southern California, from an RV site owned by a good friend who has welcomed us to stay as long as we want. I have always been blessed for having good friends that have helped me get through life. My wife and soulmate Julie is of course my closest friend; we have been together for fifty years. Not bad considering that when we got married everyone said it would never last. Amazing what love can overcome.

What am I doing now? What I consider my first priority: my family. We are blessed to have three happily married children

who have given us eight grandchildren. We try to see them as much as possible.

When I was doing Latin Fest I knew it would soon come to an end, so I'd started to look for another source of income. At that time I was asked for some advice by my friend Peter Barnett, who was setting up a lounge for crew members from cruise ships docking in Vancouver. There was a need for such a service and Peter's crew lounge immediately became very successful. I realized there was the same need in Victoria, and my son Damian suggested we should open one up. With a lot of work and financial investment, it worked out very well for the first three years. But it all came tumbling down, along with the one in Vancouver, when we were told we could no longer operate behind the customs line at the pier. It would appear that our "homeland security" authorities considered it a risk to have crew members from different ships mingling with each other before they cleared customs. When I reflect back it does seem ironic that two successful businesses I started both got shut down by government regulations.

So now what to do? We owned a large selection of posters and I believed there was a market for them. The only reason most of these are still in existence was that Julie had saved them. She started to restore some of them and we decided we would call them Afterthought Digitally Restored Posters. We then purchased equipment to reproduce them. Gary Anderson of Turntable Records in Victoria was the first to supply us with posters. As we became known, other friends would contact us with their posters. One friend, Mike Mitchell from Nanaimo, had a large collection of posters, both local and international.

Over the years, this would turn into a full-time business, though it was a financial struggle at the beginning. One of our most loyal customers was Hemp & Company, based in Victoria (www. hempandcompany.com), who manufacture and sell hemp clothing. We would put our poster images on their tee-shirts. Another was Epicure, also in Victoria (www.epicureselections.com), who produce and sell spices through home parties. Our largest account, though, was with Earthlimits, the brainchild of Sonny

Hancock, a fellow rock promoter and club owner in Philly and Jersey who is on a mission to keep our music heritage alive. It took a while for me to figure it out that he was right, and in time the posters and more were being printed under the Earthlimits banner. Most of the running of the equipment in the last few years has been done by Sonny's son, Dylan. But Dylan has decided to further his education, so Julie and I will continue to run Afterthought Enterprises and produce digitally restored reproductions of our posters.

Now with my wife and family by my side, I spend my time helping with two non-profit societies. The first is Music Heals, set up by Peter Barnett's son David. This society works to get music therapy into hospitals, palliative care hospices, seniors homes and other sites to help with healing. The other, a foundation to help BC youth in crisis, was established by Julie's Aunt Rina and is overseen by her cousin.

Who knew all those years ago where a coffeehouse in a church hall would lead?!

◄ *Frank Lewis and Jerry Kruz*

Poster 88 ▲

GASTOWN: OUR FOUNDING FAMILY

Gassy Jack Deighton arrived in what is now Vancouver on a sultry afternoon in October 1867. He had paddled around from New Westminster with an Indian guide, his Indian bride, their tiny son, the "Earl of Granville," her mother, her female cousin, an old yellow dog, two chickens and most important – one barrel of whiskey.

He had come to service the thirsts of the workers from Stamp's Mill, half a mile away (situated at what is now Centennial Pier). The mill workers helped him set up his shack on the waterfront in virgin forest at the intersection of Carrall and Water streets.

From there he conducted business in a loud-mouthed, foul-tongued, devil-may-care, good-humoured, open-handed manner. Before law came to his Gastown, he kept order among his burly customers with a whiskey barrel bung starter – the peacemaker of the new West!

Who was this man, Jack Deighton? The I Ching said on that day he was "Lu, the Wanderer."

> When a man is a wanderer and stranger, he should not be gruff nor overbearing. He must be cautious and reserved; in this way he protects himself from evil. If he is obliging toward others, he wins success.

The top line of his hexagram is the most significant. It states:

> The Bird's nest burns up.
> The wanderer laughs at first,
> Then must needs lament and weep.
> Through carelessness he loses his cow.
> Misfortune.

Here the cow represents "modesty and adaptability." The I Ching also states that the symbol for misfortune is the bird burning in its own nest. Hence the heron rising out of the burning forest. For, after Gastown had developed to the size shown in 1886, it was levelled completely by the "Great Fire." All was lost! Mother Nature weeps above the flames, ever lamenting the continuing scorching of her earth. After the fire the real estate agents and moneylenders set up business in the hollow of a burned-out tree. Sales were brisk and Vancouver was on its way.

The Indian guide, who ran away after arriving at the campsite, is blessed with good fortune:

> He would not listen to the mild ruler,
> But chose to follow the benevolent
> will of the Great Spirit.

In Salish the "Great Spirit" is in the form of the Thunderbird.

Gassy Jack's wife is the perfect symbol of the ever-continuing flow of life – Woman – the perpetuity of the species. Here, she is the tree of life – feet firmly anchored in the earth, then rising to the doves flying from her fingertips, these being the delicate beauty of thought and senses, continuing outward to the constellation Virgo, then out again to the endless cosmos and – Infinity!

The old woman sits reflecting on another time, when the Indian lived in awe and respect of the environment, one rhythm within another. Her I Ching is stated simply:

After Completion – the evolution of T'ai – Peace. The transition from confusion to order is complete. This hexagram indicates the conditions of a time of climax, which necessitates the utmost caution.

Here, the woman is moving from the old way of life into the new. The ancient sign 氒 means crossing the great stream" into a new consciousness.

The young girl is youth, forever receptive and virile. Her dream is of the shaman (medicine man) pounding out on his drum the changes and rhythms of the eternal music – the individual drumbeat that we all march to in our souls.

Between the spheres of aggression and receptivity lies the ever-constant flow of nature evolving. The circle is complete. This, then, is our founding family!

— Frank Lewis, 1971

APRIL 23, 2006: RIVER ROCK CASINO RESORT, VANCOUVER (RICHMOND)

BO DIDDLEY

While reviewing the first edit of this book I was also reading David Szatmary's book on the social history of rock and roll, *Rockin' in Time*. Frankly, it surprised me to learn how much occurred in the history of music in just that one decade from 1955 to 1965. The book gave credit for the birth of rock to just three people: B.B. King, Chuck Berry and Bo Diddley.

I felt very fortunate to have met Bo Diddley when my friend Matt Laundrie was promoting a concert by Bo at the River Rock Casino Resort in Vancouver. I was able help with the event. The day of the concert I managed to arrange a meeting with Bo for the following day. I felt

Poster 89 ➤

~HIGH TIDE ENTERTAINMENT PRESENTS~
THE LEGENDARY HALL OF FAMER...
BO DIDDLEY
~WITH~
BRICKHOUSE
Tickets
$43.50
PLUS SERVICE CHARGES
RIVER ROCK CASINO SHOW THEATRE
RICHMOND, BC
APRIL 23, 2006
8:00 PM
TICKETS AVAILABLE THROUGH TICKETMASTER AT 604-280-4444 OR WWW.TICKETMASTER.CA
PRINTED IN CANADA
POSTER DESIGN by BOB MASSE & SCOTTY C ~ 2006

very honoured to be able to spend some time with a living legend who had played such a big part in rock history. I feel he was never given the recognition he deserved. Like any fan I asked him if he would sign a few of the posters designed for the event by Bob Masse. When I asked Bo what he would like in return, I was very surprised when he said he would like a set of the Afterthought posters for his house. Apparently he had lost all of his psychedelic posters in the Hurricane Katrina flooding in New Orleans the previous summer. I was honoured to give him a set. It was shortly after this meeting that he passed away. What a great man.

REFLECTIONS 2013

I am sitting on a deck looking out over the Pacific Ocean and reflecting on my life. I am now officially retired but strangely enough I am now busier than I ever was in my working life. I am celebrating my life of survival. Our family now numbers seventeen. We are fortunate to be having a second family reunion only eight months after our first one. It is indeed a wonderful experience, hard to describe in words. In the background I hear my son talking on the phone to a friend in Victoria, describing the reunion as "organized chaos" but in a very loving way. I watch from the deck as all our grandchildren get ready to go to the beach. It is a perfect day.

My eldest granddaughter, Tyesa, wants to know whether I am coming to the beach with them. This time, in this moment, is indeed the most important, but regardless I continue to dwell on the past.

My eldest daughter, Celeste, has often asked why I focus so much on the sixties. As she aptly pointed out, that era represents only about 10 percent of my life, considering my age. I thought she had a good point. But I also realized I was not alone in my obsession with that time, as many of my peers do the same. That is, the ones that are still alive to talk about it.

It came to me that when I was young I never thought I would ever be old enough to reflect on the past. I thought I would be dead. As Julie has pointed out many times, I had many, many brushes with death. Perhaps that is why I am selective about memories of our past. As a child I was told by my mother that it was a miracle I was alive, because at birth I was a breech baby that had to be taken out with forceps. I had a broken arm and a fractured skull. It was an interesting way to come into the world. I think about the many near-death experiences that punctuated my life and I realize that if I had not been blessed to have others help me change my ways, I would not be here today reflecting on life and my wonderful family.

During the research for this book I was able to meet many friends from the past who also survived. Unfortunately it appears that many did not make it. For all of our ideals, we had a lot of unnecessary deaths. Had they lived I wonder how many more families we would have from that time?

One of the more positive contributions I feel the sixties made was its desire for peace on earth. I feel very strongly that the US war on Vietnam ended because of the protests of the sixties. I remember marching at the Vancouver courthouse against the war. It would only be a few more years before I would be at that same courthouse being sentenced to jail for "possession of cannabis." Never did I think I would end up in jail for what I believed in. Maybe Jim Morrison of The Doors had it right in his song "Strange Days."

And of course, we are still having wars, people are still going to jail for what they believe in and there are still victimless offences being punished. Yet somehow the world does change, ever so slowly, improving a little bit at a time.

Now that I am officially retired, what I enjoy most is spending time with my large family and working with the charitable foundations so close to my heart, and when I have a chance, reprinting all these restored posters. Should you want to order any of the ones featured in this book, just drop us a line at afterthoughtbook@gmail.com. I'd also like to invite you to drop by for a virtual visit at afterthoughtbook.com.

I guess what I really mean to say is that, in spite of everything that has happened, I am still a promoter at heart!

Afterwords

...THE AFTERTHOUGHT

BY BRUCE DOWAD

I still recall that momentary vision amidst thick, heady smells of incense: light show projectionists scurry about the balcony, flooding the dance floor in a magical spell of liquid light … long-haired, bushy men and ornately dressed women dance wildly, their hands, arms, legs, heads swirling to musical sounds thundering out from the stage. Unfamiliar faces. Trippers. Perhaps some US draft dodgers. Or just those more worldly ones you'd rarely, if ever, see walking downtown Vancouver streets, now drawn out of their West Coast woodwork to congregate and make revelry … a cacophony of creative energy converging as one kinetic force … the Afterthought, that often dark and mysterious place laden with alternative realities … in that moment, it was beautiful.

THE UNITED EMPIRE LOYALISTS, 1965–1970

BY JEFF RIDLEY

The story began in the fall of 1965, when five 16-year-old boys came together to form a rock band: Mike Trew, lead singer and keyboards; Anton "Tom" Kolstee, lead guitar; Jeff Ridley, rhythm guitar; Bruce Dowad, bass; and Dick Cruickshank, drums. The band's initial repertoire consisted of tunes by the Rolling Stones, the Kinks, the Young Rascals, the Kingsmen and other, similarly rough-edged material. The name of the band was the Molesters. We started playing gigs at the Afterthought at the Pender Auditorium, a club owned by Jerry Kruz, who was also our manager.

1966 Early in the year, Jerry booked the Tom Northcott Trio for a gig at the Afterthought. He wanted us to open but he didn't like the name the Molesters, so Anton came up with the name United Empire Loyalists. Lloyd Smith, owner of a head shop on Fourth Avenue in Kitsilano, designed Union Jack blazers for the band. With a new name and flashy outfits, the UEL took their first big step forward.

Our next major step came when we fired Mike Trew. Unfortunately this left us without a lead singer, but this problem was solved, for a time at least, by a beatnik from Toronto named John Lome. He lived in the famous Peace House, at 3148 Point Grey Road, which is where we practised for the short time John was with us.

The Grateful Dead made their first appearance in Vancouver in August 1966 at the Trips Festival, which also featured Big Brother & The Holding Company with Janis Joplin, and novelist Ken Kesey & The Merry Pranksters. Jerry managed to book the Dead for a concert the following week at the Afterthought. We opened the show. During the week between the Trips Festival and the Afterthought gig we hung out with the Dead at the motel they were staying at, and Jerry Garcia coached Anton with his guitar playing.

Toward the end of 1966 Rick Enns, who had been the bass player for the Tom Northcott Trio, found himself without a gig, since the trio had disbanded. Anton invited Rick to join the UEL as lead singer. As Rick was also an excellent bass player, it was only a matter of time before our original bass player, Bruce Dowad, seeing the writing on the wall, would leave the band. The UEL were now a quartet: Rick Enns, lead vocals and bass; Anton Kolstee, lead guitar; Jeff Ridley, rhythm guitar; and Dick Cruickshank, drums. And it was with this new lineup that the Loyalists really began to develop their distinctive look and sound.

We rehearsed daily in the basement of Rick's mother's house on West Tenth Avenue in Dunbar. We started each rehearsal with an extended jam. We concentrated on original material, even incorporating the "Spring Rounds" section of Stravinsky's *The Rite of Spring* into our song "Buffalo Wilkie."

In late 1966 we decided to record. We booked time in Robin Spurgin's studio and recorded "No, No, No," a Willie Cobb blues number whose actual title is "You Don't Love Me," and produced a 45 single with "Afraid of the Dark," written by Rick, on the B side. Jerry Garcia had taught us the lick to "No, No, No" during the Dead's first visit to Vancouver.

1967 In February Country Joe & The Fish made their first appearance in Vancouver for a three-night stint. We opened for them on the third night. Apparently Country Joe liked us, because when they returned a month later, we opened for them on all three nights. Joe taught us the riff that we later made into a song called "The Otis Redding Jam." You can compare our version to Country Joe's "Rock and Soul Music."

In the summer that year, the infamous Abe Snidanko busted our manager, Jerry, for possession of marijuana. Ted Rowbotham became our new manager and we played gigs in Gibson's, Nanaimo and Victoria. Meanwhile, with Jerry in jail and the Afterthought closed, Roger Schiffer opened the Retinal Circus on Davie Street, which became the new hip live music venue.

Towards late 1967 CBC Television produced a series of experimental late-night shows called *Enterprise*. One episode was devoted to British Zen philosopher Alan Watts. The producer devoted another full episode to the United Empire Loyalists. We played to a live studio audience and were videotaped chatting informally around a coffee table. The music segments of the show were given psychedelic post-production effects, some of which were quite avant garde at the time. Two of the songs from the *Enterprise* show can be heard on our 1998 CD *Notes from the Underground*.

1968 June was one of major high points in the Loyalists' career, when Cream played in Vancouver at the Pacific Coliseum and we were the opening act.

Drummer Richard Cruickshank left the band and was replaced briefly by Ted Lewis (aka Duris Maxwell), who quickly decided the Loyalists' style was not for him. Fortunately we found another drummer, Glen Hendrickson, formerly of the Black Snake Blues Band. With Glen's drumming style the Loyalists' sound evolved further. We played on bills with many top visiting bands such as the Siegel Schwall Band, Canned Heat, Steve Miller, John Handy, Peanut Butter Conspiracy, The Youngbloods, Notes from the Underground and Easy Chair. A gig with Bo Diddley was scheduled but didn't happen, because Bo Diddley's band couldn't get across the border. Handbills advertising the gig still exist and are popular with collectors.

After Siegel Schwall's visit to Vancouver, Corky Siegel invited Anton to join his band. Anton quit the Loyalists with the intention of moving to Chicago to start rehearsals for Siegel Schwall's proposed blues symphony to be performed with the San Francisco Symphony under Seiji Ozawa. When Anton left for Chicago, though, he was turned back at the border and his plan to join the Siegel Schwall Band had to be abandoned. At this point Anton decided to go back to school, where he eventually earned a PhD in ethnomusicology for his work with the aboriginal music of the Pacific Northwest. Jeff too decided to go back to school, leaving only Rick and Glen. They teamed up with Joe Mock to form Mock Duck, which enjoyed considerable success.

1969–70 In late 1969 Rick, Jeff and Glen decided to give the Loyalists another go, this time as a trio. Three songs from the trio, recorded at Robin Spurgin's studio, can be heard on the *Notes from the Underground* CD: "Lookin' and Searchin'" (three-piece), "Wait a Minute Jim" and "My Chances for Living." But with the Retinal Circus and the Afterthought both gone now, the Loyalists trio found themselves playing in dives and strip clubs. After less than a year Rick decided to try other things and left the group, thus ending this chapter of the story of the United Empire Loyalists. Thirty years later another chapter would begin, but that's a story to be told at another time.

TOM NORTHCOTT

BY PATRICK DOYLE

Tom Northcott, a musician who now lives in Kamloops, BC, first met Jerry Kruz when Jerry was trying to get Tom to sing at a club Jerry had organized in a church hall. "He was one of those indescribable characters," Northcott remembers. "Almost gnomish… but warm and very likeable. Now I don't do church-type music," Northcott said, "but I went and there were maybe 50 or 60 people there… a unique experience."

Northcott, who would go on to record for Warner Brothers in Hollywood, headed a trio under his own name and played a style of music he describes as "jazz-pop-rock" in the folk revival of the late 1950s to late 1960s. It was an era influenced by commercial folk groups like the Kingston Trio, started in the San Francisco Bay area in 1954 by Dave Guard, Bob Shane and Nick Reynolds; the Limeliters, formed in 1959 by Lou Gottlieb, Alex Hassilev and Glenn Yarbrough; and the Chad Mitchell Trio, consisting of Chad Mitchell and Mike Pugh from Washington state together with Mike Kobluk from Trail, BC. The folk boom also grew out of the Cold War, the civil rights movement and eventually the Vietnam war and was heavily involved in anti-war protests and a countercultural ethos. Under the growing influence of rock and roll the folkies went electric. Even counterculture icon Bob Dylan turned, and suddenly hardcore crowds at venues like the 1965 Newport (R.I.) Folk Festival were booing Dylan "for going electric."

"I had grown up with a very different kind of music," Northcott recounted. "I sang in the choir at the United church, listened to pop singers on the radio in the '50s." But there was no going back and soon the psychedelic side of the music started to permeate the west coast scene. "When I hit puberty, rock and roll had already been around for a while and we all went electric," says Northcott. "I loved it! We were made for each other."

Northcott credits Vancouver radio legend Tom Peacock, who died in 2006, for giving him his big break. "He put me in touch with Warner Brothers and the next thing I knew they sent me tickets to Los Angeles and $500," he said. In California he got involved with another Tom – Tom "Big Daddy" Donahue, a pioneering rock radio disc jockey, record producer and concert promoter who predicted the rise of alternative FM radio and the demise of the top-40 format in a 1967 *Rolling Stone* article titled "AM Radio Is Dead and Its Rotting Corpse Is Stinking Up the Airwaves."

What followed for Northcott was a dizzying rise. "I was playing with people like the Jefferson Airplane at the Matrix in San Francisco," he said. "It was definitely part of the whole peace, love and end of war scene, of all nature reconnecting ... I was born in 1943. I grew up in the Eisenhower era, I was an air cadet, but I never felt part of 'the machine,'" he says nostalgically about his life, contrasted to the quiet life he now leads in Kamloops.

"I am definitely diffident about my non-entity. I relish it but I would still like to be discovered," says the man who still writes songs in his head, drawing on influences ranging from the psychedelic beat-era poets and thinkers to 13th century Sufi mystic and poet Rumi. "I consider myself a recovering artist – it's a healthier addiction."

SEEDS OF TIME

BY ROCKET NORTON

It was the spring of 1965 and the British Invasion had established a firm beachhead on our shores. If it hadn't been for the American counter-strike, led by Motown of Detroit and the Beachboys of California, it would have been the musical, and cultural, subjugation of us all. For the impressionable teenagers of Vancouver, BC, the din of the battle had sent us all to rock and roll heaven.

I was 14 years old and in Grade 9 at Sir Winston Churchill High School. We were so delighted with what we were hearing that a bunch of us formed a band. We were originally the Surfs, then the Statics and after that the Aztecs. We mostly played the English mods and rockers: Zombies, Who, Pretty Things, Yardbirds, bands like that. We even had trendy mod uniforms: white slacks and white turtle-neck with dark blue blazers – very boss. By June 1966 we had survived our first year as a group and we were ready for headier things… we became the Seeds of Time and my life would never be never the same.

And something scary was happening over in the sleepy old Vancouver neigh-bourhood of Kitsilano. A young entre-preneur named Jerry Kruz opened a mu-sic hall in the small Russian Community Centre on Fourth Avenue at Arbutus Street. He called it the Afterthought. Another band had appeared on the scene at Churchill, the United Empire Loyalists, who proved themselves to be miles ahead of us by being the first act to perform at the Afterthought.

Like many revolutions, it's difficult to say exactly how it started or when the first salvo was fired, but it didn't take long for illumi-nated youth of the sixties to understand that the Afterthought was where it was at and for it to become the front line in the war on the establishment! The Afterthought was a beacon, a light in the dark. It was the Promised Land, and to those of us look-ing for answers, it was the top of the moun-tain. Pretty soon, bands from San Francisco were showing up. The best of these was Country Joe & The Fish. I saw them at the

Afterthought and I knew we'd never be mod again. The hippies had landed!

On January 13, 1967, the Seeds of Time scored our first booking at the Afterthought. We had created a rather hip repertoire of songs by rather hip groups like the Blues Project, Paul Butterfield Blues Band and Buffalo Springfield, and we were mostly accepted by the rather hip hippies gathered there that night. While we played, the hippies danced in wide whirly-bird circles, oblivious to our pres-ence. I sensed that this was somehow a compliment. To complete the strange, al-most eerie ambience, there was a light show set up in the balcony, projecting co-loured lights, slides and even movies on the walls, on the dancers and on us.

At this time the Seeds of Time was com-prised of a couple of guitarists from school who knew their destiny was in something not musical. The rest of us – Steve Walley on bass, John Hall on organ and me, Rocket Norton, on drums – were prepared to go wherever the music took us. We all knew this organically, without ever dis-cussing it. And it was our next appearance at the Afterthought that sealed that fate for us and a few others.

On the first weekend of March 1967 the Afterthought featured the Seeds of Time and a great band from New Westminster called William Tell & The Marksmen. The Marksmen played Friday, March 3, and we followed the next night. Their guitarist,

Lindsay Mitchell, was amazing and their lead singer, Geoff Edington, was the first "rock star" I had ever seen (even though the term had not yet been invented). The weekend would prove to be both prophetic and somewhat magical, as the two bands ultimately merged to form the basis of a thirty-year career more or less together, with another twenty years individually after that. Lindsay and Geoff joined the Seeds of Time and we survived the first ten years pretty much intact through the worst (or best) of the drug- and booze-blurred sixties and seventies.

What makes our union even more astonishing is how we came together that weekend at the Afterthought. Before our set on Saturday night our bassist, Steve, wandered up into the balcony to dig the Addled Chromish light show in operation. Addled Chromish was run by a guy named Jeff Lilly, assisted by his sister Jocelyn and some really freaky cats named Stephen, Kevin and Ron as well as a charismatic fellow named David who would very soon after change his name to the Reverend David the Candle Maker.

Steve was groovin' to the opening band and the fantastic lighting effects when an unsteady figure lunged at him out of the shadows. A knife blade flashed in the beam of a projector. Steve jumped aside and the assailant tumbled over a seat. The knife was jarred loose and bounced away down the steps. Not easily shaken, the ultra-cool Steve merely took a step back and lit up a cigarette. The attacker struggled to get up. He mumbled something and took a powerful but poorly aimed swing which didn't come close to its target. The lights flashed and Steve saw that it was Geoff Edington, William Tell himself. Geoff cursed and pointed a reproachful fist at Steve. It was then that Steve realized that Geoff was blind drunk. He crushed out his cigarette and offered Geoff a hand. At first Geoff snarled at it but within a few moments shrugged and grasped the peace offering. As Steve pulled him to his feet Geoff accused Steve of stealing his girlfriend. When they realized that indeed they were both going with the same girl, dismissive shrugs and laughter filled the night. The two musicians started talking and didn't stop... ever! Both of them dumped the girlfriend and Geoff joined the Seeds of Time.

Geoff Edington, Lindsay Mitchell, Steve Walley, John Hall and Rocket Norton became brothers born at the Afterthought on Fourth Avenue. We had a pact that when one of us died the rest would meet him at the Afterthought at 8 p.m. on July 1. Sadly, Steve Walley passed away recently, and for the first time in our lives we will gather there this year.

JERRY GARCIA ON PLAYING THE AFTERTHOUGHT

FROM *MOJO-NAVIGATOR R&R NEWS* (1966) AS CITED IN RELATED READING SECTION AT "GRATEFUL DEAD INTERVIEW."

Mojo: You played that Trips Festival in Vancouver, didn't you?

Garcia: Right.

M: What was it like?

G: It was kind of funny. Stiff, is what it was. And the people are a certain kind of reserved.

M: Who was there besides you and Big Brother?

G: The Daily Flash and some local band, I don't remember what their name was. The Painted Ship, I believe. And the PH Phactor Jug Band.

M: How did they react to the San Francisco sound?

G: Well, actually we did much better on the next weekend, when we played again at another dance, and had a fairly good crowd; but it was really good, you know, it was responsive. Much more so than the Trips Festival, because the Trips Festival wasn't really a Trips Festival; it was just a light show... a very complex light show, but in terms of what it did with the music it was pretty meaningless also. The whole thing didn't work out, being not very together, you know. It was more like there was one thing happening on the screen, there was another thing happening on the stage. [The whole event] wasn't very well run, and it wasn't well conceived, and it was mostly done by people who weren't very experienced at it. So it wasn't really... the way I see it is the amount of money they spent they would have done better by, you know, using what they had in a little bit more intelligent way. They would do things like have every band every night, so a band would only get to play maybe one set a night and it would be a short one. You couldn't really get warmed up, you know, or get any kind of thing going. It wasn't really much fun to play. The next weekend was much better.

THE WOODSTOCK CONNECTION

BY JULIA BIDEN KRUZ

I met Jessie in Vancouver on our first day of Grade 8. She, her twin brother and her sister had just arrived in town from northern BC. We soon became best friends and spend most of our free time hanging out together.

Jessie and I were regulars at the Afterthought and she was soon dating Jerry's best friends and we would all hang out together. By the end of 1966 she and I were both attending UBC, Jessie in linguistics and I in education. By 1968 I had left university but Jessie continued on to finish her degree and then left Vancouver to travel in Europe. Upon her return we renewed our friendship and continued to move in the same social circles.

By the time the summer of 1969 arrived, Jerry and I were married and expecting our first child. Jessie had left for the summer to explore Canada. That summer we all heard rumours about this great festival that was going to be held in New York state and how all the great bands of the time were going to perform. All one had to do was to get to New York state and to a small town called Woodstock.

Jessie by this time had reached Montreal and met up with fellow hippies who were intent on getting to the festival. She hooked up with a nice young man and they hitchhiked to Woodstock, getting there in time to enjoy the event. Jessie says she remembers standing on the hill and seeing a photographer snapping pictures but at the time was more concerned with being tired and cold. So imagine her surprise when the Woodstock record album was released and there she is on the cover. The quilt covering them she had had for years, a gift from her grandmother. Her rose-colored glasses were ones she had been wearing only a few months. When Jessie returned to Vancouver we all marvelled that of all the pictures that must have been taken at the festival, the one with Jessie in it had been chosen to represent Woodstock.

Many years later (in fact it was *Life* magazine's 20th anniversary issue), another couple were trotted out as being the couple on the cover, now happily married and raising two children. Another couple somewhere else in the US also said they were the ones. Needless to say, Jessie was

not happy about this and contacted the magazine, sending pictures of herself at the time. There are still questions about who the Woodstock couple were, and the Rock & Roll Hall of Fame has refused to display this iconic photograph until the matter is resolved.

All of us who knew Jessie back in the day, though, are convinced that this photograph is her.

PAUL DEYONG

BY PATRICK DOYLE

"We used to provide sound and PA for the big names when they came to town," says Paul Deyong offhandedly. He rhymes off some of the groups: Tina Turner, the Platters, Zappa & The Mothers of Invention, Chuck Berry…

"Chuck Berry was a brilliant musician," Deyong warms to the topic. "He liked to come to Vancouver because we made him sound better than anywhere else. Groups like the Platters – that was music from the '50s, they didn't need the big sound… it wasn't needed for a song like "My Girl" [by the Temptations]… A thousand watts was considered big back then, and Vancouver had it when it came to sound. Chuck Berry said the biggest reason he liked to come here was our sound… we built custom stuff for him to take away."

Deyong said he got into the business of working with rock bands almost by accident. "I was selling stereo systems – JBL speakers, they were the only ones that could handle the kind of bass these guys put out. The loudest thing you could get at the time was a Fender amp, and they were pretty lame," he said.

Deyong said the nightclub scene helped keep the music alive between the concerts featuring the big names. He rattles off a list of the west coast clubs that influenced the scene: Oil Can Harry's, The Cave, the Paloma, and a club run by a kid named Kruz, the Afterthought. He credits the young impresario with knowing "a lot more about the music business at the time." Deyong describes the era as a "pivot point" for music in Vancouver. "It was a between

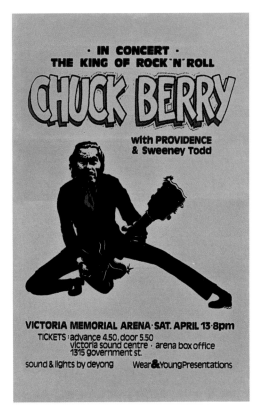

▲ *One of the many big fans of Deyong audio.*

time. Jerry knew it. He knew it was a pivot point and he was there."

He remembers Kruz and Jeffrey Barnett worked to make psychedelic posters for the acts that were playing in the burgeoning music scene in Vancouver in the late '60s and early '70s. For Deyong, however, sound was the big thing. "At the time, you have got to remember, there weren't a lot of powerful amplifiers to be found… people were using home hi-fi. Vancouver got a reputation for giving sound that you couldn't get in a lot of the US… they had to come up here if they wanted to get more air." He explained, "A cleaner bass required stereo to get that quality."

Deyong said that even acts not known for "big sound" liked to come to Vancouver for the quality. "Even Tiny Tim wanted what we had. He wanted clarity." He chuckles and concedes that the acts had at least one other reason for favouring Canada's west coast scene: "Grass! It was easier to get grass here… that and the concerts."

VANCOUVER ROCK RADIO

BY JERRY KRUZ

I am sitting on our balcony with Julie and a dear friend, Pam Burge. Pam was kind enough to come over from Vancouver to tell this story about the Vancouver radio scene in the '60s. We reminisced about old times and how things had changed.

Pam's name was Tim Burge when we first met and at that time was an up-and-coming radio DJ in Vancouver who was prepared to take chances by playing what became known as psychedelic music. At last there was someone on the air that understood the music I was trying to bring to the masses. Tim was on CKLG, one of only two radio stations in those days that played rock and roll. It was a cutting-edge time for the kind of music that today is the rule rather than the exception.

Sometime in the fall of 1966, thanks to my association with Tim, I would start to advertise on 'LG. I had always thought it was CKLG FM, but I was corrected by Pam that 'LG FM didn't start up until March 1968. I do believe Tim was the first in the city to play the music I was promoting, and it would take about a year and a half before psychedelic rock would become mainstream. On CJOR in the fall of '67 he would be the first to play Country Joe's "Section 43," a song about eight minutes long, which was unheard of at the time.

Tim would play "Section 43" and then the flip side, "Sweet Lorraine."

I had just returned from Montreal and it was a great treat to hear Tim play music on the radio that in 1965 and '66 I was told would never make it to radio. How times have changed. I believe it was Tim who first interviewed Country Joe & The Fish and the Grateful Dead on the air. Tim would take musical chances that no one else would take, and it would eventually cost him his job. He was fired from CJOR in December 1967, then hired back by CKLG FM in about April 1968. 'LG would turn out to be one of the first FM stations in North America to depart from traditional Top 40 programming. While I thought it took a long time for psychedelic music to become mainstream, Pam pointed out that two years was not really very long, considering the whole lifespan of rock and roll.

I recall the times when I would be in the studio with Tim while he was on air live. As he was talking I believed all the youth of Vancouver were listening. I believe that Tim Burge must have had something to do with growing attendance of the Afterthought

As I sit on our deck with Pam, we reflect on what we both have been through and are thankful we are both alive to talk about it. I realize that what I had to deal with does not begin to compare to what Pam has had to handle. I want to give credit to her for changing the face of music on the airwaves of Vancouver.

HYDROGEN SALES

BY BILL DOGH

(Jerry: *We met Bill through our good friend Theresa "Bitty" Neel. Bitty was our poster distributor for the Afterthought, and every week she and Bill would put up Afterthought posters throughout Vancouver.*)

Hydrogen Sales was formed in the spring of 1968 as a result of a meeting with Frank Lewis. Frank, along with King Anderson and another artist who did one poster, had produced a series of posters in 1967 to be sold at the Teen Fair, which was a popular attraction that had been held at the Armoury the previous year (see posters 63–71, beginning opposite page 142). Frank at that time had all the unsold posters from that year's Teen Fair, and Brian Peterson, my business partner who introduced me to Frank, arranged to get a number of these from Frank on credit. When we returned to pay Frank and buy some more posters, Frank took an interest in our sales efforts and was very co-operative and helpful to us, as the "psychedelic" style was a new form of poster art which was received by the general public with mixed enthusiasm. Some stores absolutely refused to handle them, while others enthusiastically added them to their inventories.

At that time, the best-known Vancouver psychedelic poster artist was Bob Masse, whose works were wholesaled by his partner Bob Hogler under the firm name Organic Arts. When Bob Hogler closed out Organic Arts to return to his family's business, we purchased his remaining stock of Bob Masse posters and added them to our line of Frank Lewis and King Anderson posters.

By late 1969 the novelty of locally produced psychedelic posters had waned to the point that we simply closed up shop and put our unsold (but paid for) inventory in storage.

CRISIS CENTRE MEMORIES, VANCOUVER

BY GIL HENRY

(**Jerry:** *I met up with Gil Henry while picking up our respective grandchildren at their school in Victoria. We had often crossed paths there, but had not spoken to each other until Penny Barner (the school's administrator) told me that Gil and I should have a lot in common, as we were both in Vancouver at the same time. And it turned that Gil had worked for Alexandra Neighbourhood House at the same time that I served on its board of directors while I was attending college. Gil today continues his career as principal of Selkirk Montessori School in Victoria, BC.*)

I was living at Fourth and Trafalgar in the late '60s and early '70s, newly married to Angela. I was a student at both UBC and SFU in education. During those years, to help pay the bills, I was also a volunteer and later a supervisor at the Vancouver Crisis Centre at Alexandra Neighbourhood House at Seventh and Burrard. Many volunteers were trained there to work the telephones and counsel people in crisis. There were also phones dedicated to youth in need. This focus of the centre was called NOW. Volunteer crisis counsellors in NOW were specially trained to deal with youth, and in particular in "talking down" bad drug trips.

There were a number of other services too that emerged during this time to support young people. A drop-in centre was created on the main floor of Alexandra House. The most significant service, however, was the big yellow NOW bus decorated in a psychedelic motif. Most of the seats were removed and the bus became a mobile counselling/medical centre. It travelled to all the events where youth would gather, including concerts and the Be-Ins Jerry Kruz organized at Stanley Park. Volunteer doctors were on hand to provide medical help, and counsellors were ready to talk and listen to distressed kids.

These were huge events attended by the counterculture in Vancouver at that time. The live concerts attracted many and the NOW bus was on site not only to be part of the scene but to offer help to any unfortunate kid who had taken bad drugs or who was unable to navigate the mind-altered state.

We were well equipped to handle all manner of "freak-outs." The rabbit, however, was another matter. One evening, a young girl tripping badly brought her equally stoned rabbit onto the bus. We settled them both at the back of the bus, and while Angela was talking the girl down, the rabbit peed day-glo orange all over Angela's beautiful hand-knit hippie poncho!

Also around this time, the Beatty Street Drill Hall was converted to a youth hostel, where many backpackers could find a place to sleep. The NOW bus held regular medical clinics for travellers, served by volunteer doctors at sites like this.

I remember attending a rally at UBC in October 1968. Jerry Rubin, the American "yippee" leader, spoke. Once agitated and full of righteous indignation, the crowd marched to the faculty club and staged a "sit-in" which lasted throughout the night. The faculty club was regarded as the established power and we the hippies were there to "liberate the building."

AUNT RINA

BY NINA LYONS, ADMINISTRATOR OF THE
RINA M. BIDIN FOUNDATION

Rina Maria Bidin was born in Deroche, BC, in 1914 to Italian immigrants. She spent her childhood in Woodfibre, a mill town on Howe Sound accessible only by steamboat. Joseph and Lucia Bidin had seven children: Lucio, Victor and Leno (Leno would perish in a boating accident in Howe Sound at the age of 10), Rina, Mary and twins Alma and Elda (Elda, at less than a year old would die of pneumonia within a month of Leno's death).

Rina went to school in Woodfibre through Grade 7. There was no schooling available beyond that in the town, but her father believed strongly in education, so he sent Rina to Vancouver to complete Grades 8 through 12. Through various circumstances of the time, Rina met and eventually boarded with Frank and Gina Federici, who became Uncle Frank and Auntie Gina. She attended Britannia School on Napier Street.

Early on, Rina was the receptionist and bookkeeper for Uncle Frank's Hotel Vancouver barbershop. Frank eventually turned the management of the barbershop over to her, and it was through the barbershop that Rina met many of the city's and the province's influential businesspeople. These introductions eventually led to her first real estate purchase. She was forever afterwards driven by a passion for acquiring and selling properties.

In 1954 a *Toronto Star* journalist investigating BC's "crazy" new Social Credit government was getting a haircut at the barbershop. He crossed swords with Rina, who vigorously defended the premier, W.A.C. "Wacky" Bennett. Beland Honderich, later the publisher of the *Star*, persuaded Rina to continue their discussion over dinner. More than forty years later they met again, in Toronto. Eventually they married in Hawaii and Beland moved to Vancouver. They spent six happy years together until his death in 2005. During their years they shared a passion for philanthropy and common beliefs in the wellness of children and youth. Rina passed away April 16, 2011, at the age of 96.

THE RINA M. BIDIN FOUNDATION

BY NINA LYONS, ADMINISTRATOR OF THE RINA M. BIDIN FOUNDATION

Rina always enjoyed fundraising and promoting many causes among her vast network of friends and family, and she established the Rina M. Bidin Foundation in 1988. She left part of her estate to the Bidin Honderich Orphan Children's Fund, and it is the Bidin Foundation that holds those funds in trust for distribution to causes that promote the values and beliefs Rina held throughout her life.

To that end, the foundation's support is focused on BC-based and preferably already established or supportable programs with the purpose of improving the future for children and youth up to age 24. Grants are restricted to organizations recognized by the Canada Revenue Agency as "qualified donees." The foundation seeks the neediest of children and youth around the province and is committed to ensuring that First Nations children and youth are equally represented through the annual granting process.

The foundation funds programs focused on but not limited to:

- early childhood development and education

- health and wellness, including food and nutrition

- culture and language

- life skills

- educational programs

- scholarships/bursaries

- youth at risk – housing, mentoring and empowering them to live healthy, stable lives

- access to sports and physical activity

- access to arts

MUSIC HEALS

BY CHRIS BRANDT, EXECUTIVE DIRECTOR OF MUSIC HEALS

Music Heals is a Vancouver-based foundation that was formed to help raise awareness of the healing power of music and to help fundraise for music therapy and related services across British Columbia and throughout Canada. The foundation is governed by a core belief that music therapists provide an essential medical and psychological service.

Music therapy is the skillful use of music as a therapeutic tool to restore, maintain and improve mental, physical and emotional health. With generous support from individuals and from foundation and corporate donors, Music Heals is able to provide support for programs that employ music therapists in hospitals, hospices and private homes across the country. Music therapy is not funded by the federal government.

Music Heals supports music therapy programs serving patients in areas of care including children's hospitals, seniors' homes, palliative care, bereavement, autism support, burn units, AIDS and HIV support, rehabilitation and more. Priorities for funding are set by a committee of music therapists, and therefore projects are only considered upon their recommendation. Some 40 per cent of the Music

Heals board of directors is comprised of music therapists, including the past president of the Music Therapy Association of BC. Due to the wide range of programs served, the foundation is able to support the areas of care that resonate most with donors. All are deserving of program expansion. The objective is to increase access to music therapy services at a given institution by one day per week for a full year.

Institutions are selected for support based on having a well-developed and respected music therapy program that serves to provide comfort, rehabilitation, reduction of pain and anxiety, and even legacy recordings for terminal patients. Their goal is to simply increase the number of hours that this tremendous program is offered. Most institutions only have an accredited music therapist on staff for one or two days per week, and $15,000 facilitates an increase in patient access to music therapy by one day a week for a year.

Research has shown that one day per week of music therapy programming for a year will serve an additional 400 patients on average. In a program that only has a music therapist on staff for two days a week, increasing access by one day equals a 50 per cent increase in service.

Music Heals fulfills its mandate by selecting institutions that support music therapy on an ongoing basis, thereby providing incentive and positive reinforcement to continue to prioritize this form of therapy. The foundation insists that any funding it provides must serve to increase these services, not replace existing funding. Therefore the funding strategy puts the onus on the institution to continue to fund each program, so that they might match funds again in the future.

The foundation does not collect any administration fee on donor funding, and it redirects 100 per cent of the funds to the selected music therapy program. Commitments are obtained from each supported institution that all moneys received from Music Heals will be allocated entirely to their music therapy program.

Music Heals manages the iPod Pharmacy, Caring Concerts and A Night Out for Music Heals, and works in partnership with the Music Therapy Ride on the Bandwagon Project. The iPod Pharmacy collects good-as-new iPods, pairs them with new headphones from Skullcandy and iTunes gift cards paid for by Scotiabank, and delivers them to music therapists for their work with their patients. Caring Concerts is a live music series where professional musicians visit facilities and perform for patients. Neither of these initiatives are technically music therapy, but they help to raise awareness for music therapy programs and services. The Bandwagon is the world's first mobile recording studio designed specifically for music therapists. The first of its kind resides permanently in the BC Children's Hospital, and the second unit travels around the province for six-week residencies in various music therapy programs.

Join the conversation by following Music Heals on Facebook and Twitter, and by visiting www.musicheals.ca.

LES VOGT

PATRICK DOYLE

Another impresario from the era, Les Vogt, was less than impressed by the drug connection to music from the era. "All that psychedelic shit turned me off!" Vogt says. "Drugs and that entire psychedelic scene wasn't what I was into."

Vogt remembers Jerry Kruz as "a kid who used to hang around my office trying to book bands" for his nightclub, a converted dancehall which Vogt concedes had "a successful run" with the "psychedelic" crowd. Vogt says he had little time for nightclubs and bars, preferring bigger venues.

"Clubs weren't good for the business… Roy Orbison was working in Ontario in a bar with four guys in his band earning $800 a night for the whole band. I chased him down and told his manager I can book you into theatres," Vogt said of a relationship that began with a cross-Canada tour in 1976 and ended in a 10-year relationship with the superstar.

THE LAST WORD

JULIA AND COMPANY

"**Afterword**, *noun*: concluding remarks in a book, either by the author or by someone who has enjoyed the book and often has some influence or expertise in the subject matter."

In the case of this book, we know the author and we know the subject matter – one of us better than the others – but we are not influential in the field nor does anyone know who we are. Well, that's not altogether true; the author knows us. Many of the people mentioned in this book know us, but none of you, the readers, know us. Yet we know this story, these stories, and we feel as though we could conclude this book just as well as any of the famous people who are mentioned in it.

Let's start back at the beginning, way back, with a young man who had big dreams, dreams that included rock and roll and his name up in lights. Many people said he was just a kid who wanted to have some fun, and they were right: he *was* a kid, a kid who thought he could do big things.

He took those dreams and made them into a life, into the story he has shared here. It's a unique story, one that shaped the lives of the many people who would come to know Jerry Kruz, both in the years you've been reading about here and in the decades that followed.

Fifty years ago these were lived events. Now they are stored in our personal memories and have only been brought back to light in the last few years as this book was being written. Many were the nights we would sit with friends and family while Jerry would regale us with tales of the Afterthought. There were stories about the bands, the light shows, the antics of young adults who found themselves coming of age in a generation that would help define the world we live in today. We would add our memories, and our children would listen raptly as we shared what the '60s were really like. Names we knew from the music world would be dropped and we would wonder how all of this could have happened to some kid from Vancouver.

Many people could tell you about Jerry's tireless promoting, the rock posters, the travels and the epic events you've read about here. They are great stories, true stories, stories that may well have surprised you and left you wondering if they were even true. Sure, we could drop names from popular bands and famous people who know Jerry, who remember him, who played at the Afterthought and whom he stills calls friends even after all these years. But most of those people could not tell you about the person Jerry became after those years: about his continued career, his charity work or his dedication to his children and grandchildren. They could not tell you about how these stories too would shape his life and the lives of all the people who would come to know him, to call him husband, friend, father and grandfather. It has been our joy and privilege to work on this book with Jerry and to watch it grow from just a dream.

The Afterthought helped define an entire generation. We hope the stories you've experienced here have struck a chord with you and given you some insight into the lives of musicians, artists, promoters and youth who helped spark an entirely new culture in Vancouver, Canada, in the 1960s.

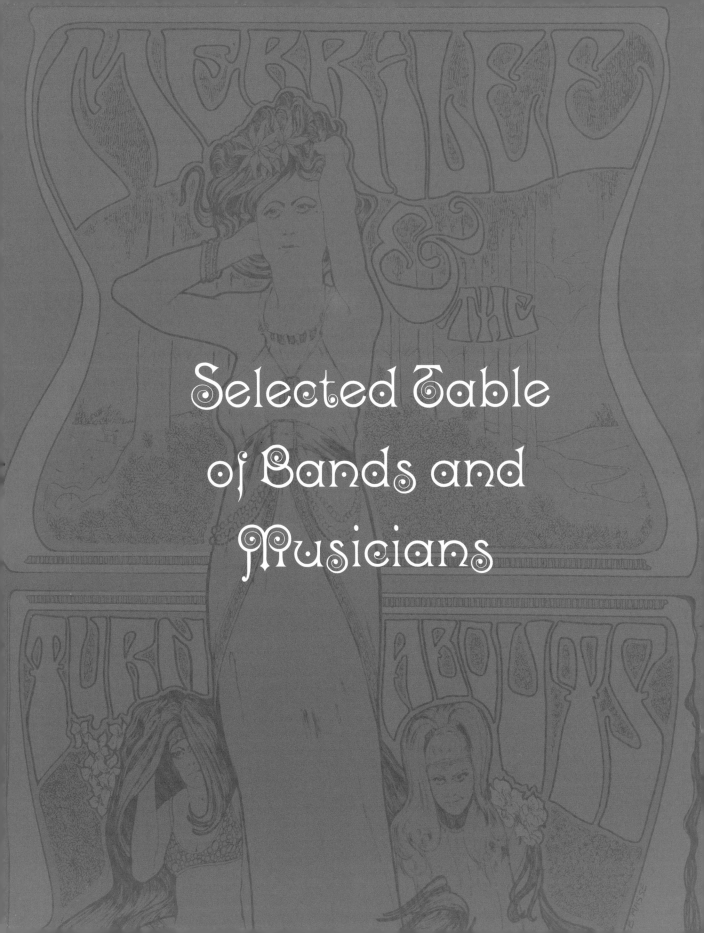

Selected Table
of Bands and
Musicians

BAND NAME ORIGINALLY	BAND NAMES LATER	PLAYERS [*ORIGINAL MEMBERS MARKED WITH ASTERISK WHERE KNOWN]	PLAYERS' OTHER BANDS, WHETHER EARLIER OR LATER
Bitter Sweets		Brian Fisher, lead vocals	
		Steve Grosvenor, lead guitar	
		Rob Deans, organ	
		Phil Smeltzer, bass	
		Lawrence Miller (aka Larry Turnquist), drums	
Black Snake Blues Band		Joe Conroy, guitar	
		Norm MacPherson, guitar	
		Pat McDonald, guitar, vocals	
		Shari Pandi, keys	
		George Chapelas, bass	Shockers, Night Train Revue, Trials of Jayson Hoover, Pirannah Bros., Shakedown
		Glen Hendrickson, drums	United Empire Loyalists, Mock Duck, Orville Dorp, Uproar, Shakedown
		Ron Flatman, drums	
		Ted Harrison, drums	
Bobby Taylor & The Vancouvers		Bobby Taylor, vocals	Little Daddy & The Bachelors
		Tommy Chong, guitar	The Calgary Shades, Little Daddy & The Bachelors
		Eddie Patterson, guitar, bass, vocals	
		Robbie King, keys	Papa Bear's Medicine Show, The Good Shepherds, Brahman, Chilliwack, Doucette, Powder Blues, Cal Batchelor Band
		Wes Henderson, bass	Roger Jerome & The Casuals, Little Daddy & The Bachelors,
		Ted Lewis (aka Duris Maxwell), drums	The Tornadoes, The Chessmen, The Good Shepherds, Little Daddy & The Bachelors, United Empire Loyalists, Privilege, Brahman, Skylark, Country Love, Heart, Doucette, Powder Blues, Johnny V; session and tour work (Eddie Money, Meatloaf, Toto)
Brave New World		*Paul Trousdale, lead vocals, songwriter	

BAND NAME ORIGINALLY	BAND NAMES LATER	PLAYERS [*ORIGINAL MEMBERS MARKED WITH ASTERISK WHERE KNOWN]	PLAYERS' OTHER BANDS, WHETHER EARLIER OR LATER
		*George M. Guilmet, keys, vocals	
		*Gus Molvik, guitar, vocals	Listen
		*Mike Beck, bass	
		*John Kennedy, drums	
		Mike Whalen, keys	
		Ron Foos, bass	Paul Revere & The Raiders
		Gary Oldroyd, bass	Annie Rose & The Thrillers
		Ron Adcock, drums	
		Bill Brammer, drums	Smoking Gun
		Randy Espeseth, drums	Baron's Blues Band
The Centaurs		*Ron Williams, vocals	
		*Hugh Reilly, guitar	Rogues
		*Louis Pitre, organ	
		*Al West, bass	Yeoman
		*John Gedak, drums	Rogues
		Chad Thorp, keys, vocals	The Nocturnals
		Bob Brown, organ	
The Classics (aka CFUN Classics)	The Collectors [see below]	Howie Vickers, trombone, vocals	The Good Shepherds, The Collectors, Chilliwack, Wildroot
		Claire Lawrence, sax, organ, flute	The Collectors, Chilliwack
		Tom Baird, keys	Roger Jerome & The Casuals
		Brian Russell, guitar	
		Glenn Miller, bass	The Collectors, Chilliwack
		Gary Taylor, drums	
		Fred Latremouille, drums	
The Coastmen		*Laurence Cable, vocals	Pennywhistle
		*Denis (Basil) Watson, keys, guitar, bass, vocals	Stallion Thumrock
		*Roman Spanier, guitar	
		*Peter Schmit, bass	
		*Brian Temple, drums	
		George Greenwell, lead guitar	Pennywhistle, Seeds of Time
		Ted Harrison, drums	Black Snake Blues Band
		Lindsay Robson, drums	Terry & The Jestrites

BAND NAME ORIGINALLY	BAND NAMES LATER	PLAYERS [*ORIGINAL MEMBERS MARKED WITH ASTERISK WHERE KNOWN]	PLAYERS' OTHER BANDS, WHETHER EARLIER OR LATER
The Collectors	*Chilliwack*	Bill Henderson, guitar	
		Claire Lawrence, sax, organ, flute	The Classics
		Howie Vickers, vocals	The Classics
		Glenn Miller, bass	The Classics
		Ross Turney, drums	
The Dimensions		*Joe Villa, guitar, vocals	
		*Lee Dark, sax, guitar, vocals,	
		*Clyde Heaton, organ, kbd bass, vocals	
		*Bill Hoak, bass	
		*Ron Villa, drums	
		Clayton Bellhimer, drums	
		Bernie Harris, vocals	
		Valerie Rosa, vocals	
		Glenn Wiest, guitar	
Don Crawford & The Right People		Don Crawford, guitar, vocals	
		Rod Evans, guitar	
		Reid Hudson, bass	
		Dennis Scherk, drums	
The Family Dogs		Walt Kowal, tambourine, vocals	
		Gordy Walker, guitar	
		Ron "Bones" "Bono" McRobbie, bass	Dynatones, Hotwire, Danny Tripper Band
		Stu Wilson, drums	Winter's Green
Fireweed		Danny Mack, guitar, vocals	Van-Dels, Banff Playboys, Danny Soul, Fantastic Sensations, Hydroelectric Streetcar, Cement City Cowboys, Danny Mack & Alberta Crude, Danny Mack & The Shuffle Dawgs
		Dan Tapanila, guitar, vocals	Painted Ship
		Danny Tripper, guitar, vocals	Dynatones, Hotwire, Danny Tripper Band
		Lee Stephens, bass, vocals	Mock Duck, Cement City Cowboys
		Stan Tait, drums	Spring

BAND NAME ORIGINALLY	BAND NAMES LATER	PLAYERS [*ORIGINAL MEMBERS MARKED WITH ASTERISK WHERE KNOWN]	PLAYERS' OTHER BANDS, WHETHER EARLIER OR LATER
The Fox		Paul Dean, guitar, vocals	Kentish Steele & The Shantelles, Canada, Scrubbaloe Caine, Streetheart, Loverboy
		Clyde Harvey, organ, lead vocals	The Statesmen, Canada
		Brian Newcombe, bass	Canada, Chilliwack
		Billy McBeth, drums, lead vocals	The Nocturnals, Canada, Scrubbaloe Caine, TR3
The Good Shepherds		Al Johnson, vocals	Roger Jerome & The Casuals, Night Train Revue
		Eddie Patterson, guitar	Brahman
		Robbie King, organ	Bobby Taylor & The Vancouvers, Papa Bear's Medicine Show, Brahman, Chilliwack, Doucette, Powder Blues
		Ronnie Banks, bass	
		Ted Lewis (aka Duris Maxwell), drums	The Tornadoes, The Chessmen, Little Daddy & The Bachelors, Bobby Taylor & The Vancouvers, United Empire Loyalists, Privilege, Brahman, Skylark, Country Love, Heart, Doucette, Powder Blues, Johnny V; session and tour work (Eddie Money, Meatloaf, Toto)
		Hans Stamer, vocals	
		Howie Vickers, vocals	The Classics, The Collectors, Chilliwack, Wildroot
The Jabberwock	*My Indole Ring*	John King, guitar	
		John Cluff, organ	
		David Jordan Knox, bass	
		Chris Dahl, drums	Cement City Cowboys
Jayson Hoover & The Epics	*Trials of Jayson Hoover*	Jayson Hoover, vocals	
		Jim Harmata, guitar	Pirannah Bros.
		Bill Gibson, keyboards	
		Gunther Klaus, saxophone	
		Bob Kidd, bass	
		Dave MacPhail, drums	

BAND NAME ORIGINALLY	BAND NAMES LATER	PLAYERS [*ORIGINAL MEMBERS MARKED WITH ASTERISK WHERE KNOWN]	PLAYERS' OTHER BANDS, WHETHER EARLIER OR LATER
Joe Mock & No Commercial Potential	*Mock Duck [see below]*	Joe Mock, guitar, vocals	Mock Duck
		David Sinclair, guitar	Sunshyne, Prism, Straight Lines, Body Electric, The Wilds, duo with Kent Fiddy, duo with Keith Bennett; also first-call session/tour player for, e.g., k.d. lang, Sarah McLachlan, Michael Bublé, BTO, Bryan Adams, Amy Sky, Rita MacNeil, Paul Janz, Valdy, Susan Jacks, Terry Jacks, Irish Rovers, Gary Fjellgaard etc.
		Spence Sutton, vibes	
		Tom Hazlett, bass	The Trenmen
		Steve Barrett, drums	
Kentish Steele & The Shantelles		Kentish Steele, vocals	
		Brian Tansley, saxophone	The Intensions
		Brian Pulham, bass	The Intensions
		Jim Patterson, drums	
		Steve Cartmell, organ	Trials of Jayson Hoover
		Brian Tingle, organ	The Intensions
		Gordon Walkinshaw, keyboards	
		Norman B. Glass, guitar	
		Paul Dean, guitar	The Fox, Canada, Scrubbaloe Caine, Streetheart, Loverboy
		Warren Clarke, trumpet	
		Gary Greensword, trumpet	
		Stu Meadows, trombone	
		Glen Gish, saxophone	
		Joni Moore, vocals	
Little Daddy & The Bachelors		Tommy "Little Daddy" Melton, vocals	The Calgary Shades
		Tommy Chong, guitar	The Calgary Shades, Bobby Taylor & The Vancouvers
		Bernie Sneed, keyboards	
		Wes Henderson, bass	The Calgary Shades, Roger Jerome & The Casuals, Bobby Taylor & The Vancouvers

BAND NAME ORIGINALLY	BAND NAMES LATER	PLAYERS [*ORIGINAL MEMBERS MARKED WITH ASTERISK WHERE KNOWN]	PLAYERS' OTHER BANDS, WHETHER EARLIER OR LATER
		Ted Lewis (aka Duris Maxwell), drums	The Tornadoes, The Chessmen, The Good Shepherds, Bobby Taylor & The Vancouvers, United Empire Loyalists, Privilege, Brahman, Skylark, Country Love, Heart, Doucette, Powder Blues, Johnny V; session and tour work (Eddie Money, Meatloaf, Toto)
		Don Mallory, drums	
		Floyd Sneed, drums	The Calgary Shades, Three Dog Night
Liverpool Five		*Steve Laine, vocals	
		*Ken Cox, guitar, vocals	
		*Ron Henley, keys, sax, vocals	
		*Freddy Dennis, bass, vocals	
		*Jimmy May, drums, vocals	
		Gary Milkie, keys	
		Mark Gage, keys	
		Dave Burgess, bass	
Mock Duck		*Joe Mock, guitar, vocals	Joe Mock & No Commercial Potential
		*Lee Stephens, bass	Fireweed, Cement City Cowboys
		*Glen Hendrickson, drums	United Empire Loyalists, Black Snake Blues Band, Orville Dorp, Uproar, Shakedown
		Rick Enns, bass, vocals	Rogues, Tom Northcott Trio, United Empire Loyalists, Seeds of Time
		Ross Barret, sax, keys	The Trenmen
Night Train Revue		Suzanne Cliff, vocals	
		Billy Dixon, vocals	
		Chuck Flintroy, vocals	
		Lovena Fox, vocals	
		Donny Gerrard, vocals	Roger Jerome & The Casuals, Trials of Jayson Hoover, Skylark
		Tony Harris, vocals	
		Chuck Hintrov, vocals	
		Al Johnson, vocals	Roger Jerome & The Casuals, The Good Shepherds
		Kenny McColl, vocals	
		Sy Risby, vocals	
		Bill Hallett, trumpet	

BAND NAME ORIGINALLY	BAND NAMES LATER	PLAYERS [*ORIGINAL MEMBERS MARKED WITH ASTERISK WHERE KNOWN]	PLAYERS' OTHER BANDS, WHETHER EARLIER OR LATER
		Paul Barron, trumpet	
		Ron Johnson, trombone	
		Dennis Esson, trombone	
		Bill Keyes, sax	
		Larry Volen, sax	Larry Volen Trio
		Wayne Morris, sax	
		Bill Wheeler, guitar	
		Lorne McGee, guitar	
		Chuck Cliff, organ	
		Ray Marquis, bass	
		George Chapelas, bass	The Shockers, Black Snake Blues Band, Trials of Jayson Hoover, Pirannah Bros., Shakedown
		Doug Cuthbert, drums	
The Nocturnals		Carl Erickson, sax	
		Roger Skinner, sax	
		Ron Henshel, guitar	
		Chad Thorp, organ	
		Wayne Evans, bass	
		Billy McBeth, drums	The Fox, Canada, Scrubbaloe Caine, TR3
Northwest Company [1965–67] aka The Electric Train [1967–68]		Newman Corey, vocals	
		Brian Barrington, guitar	Mantra
		Jeffrey Herman, keys	
		Barry Walker, bass	
		Gary Kennedy, drums	Mantra
		Graham Walker, drums	Reign
Northwest Company [1967 on]		*Rick McCartie, vocals	The Questions
		*Ray O'Toole, guitar, vocals	Blue Northern, Ray O'Toole Band, Home Cooking, Shakedown
		*Vidar Skofteby, keys, guitar, vocals	
		*Gowan Jorgenson, bass, vocals	
		*Jerry Ringrose, drums	
		Richard Stepp, drums, vocals	The Questions, Law Bros. Band, Home Cooking, Shakedown, Richard Stepp Band, Stepp & Stomp

BAND NAME ORIGINALLY	BAND NAMES LATER	PLAYERS [*ORIGINAL MEMBERS MARKED WITH ASTERISK WHERE KNOWN]	PLAYERS' OTHER BANDS, WHETHER EARLIER OR LATER
		Leslie Law, guitar	Mother Tucker's Yellow Duck, Law Bros. Band
		Dan Smith, guitar	Six Cylinder
		Zak August, guitar	
		Brent Shindell, guitar	High Flying Bird, Bruce Miller Band, Doucette
Painted Ship		*Bill Hay, vocals, harp	
		*Rob Rowden, guitar	The Look
		*Ken Wain, organ	Trials of Jayson Hoover
		*Barry Rowden, drums	The Look
		Joe Conroy, guitar	
		Danny Tapanila, guitar	Fireweed
		Barry Forrester, guitar	
		Larry Kovich, guitar	
		Jim McGillveray, drums	Wildroot
		Sharlene (Sonny), occasional tambourine	
		Barry Simpson, keyboards	
		Ken Warren, keyboards	
		Tom Keeling, keys	
		Spenser Sulton, keys	
		Gary Connor, bass	
		Chris Huntley, bass	
		Brian Kelly, bass	
		Lou Wade, drums	
		John Webber, drums	The Briars
		Dave Whiting, drums	
Papa Bear's Medicine Show		Craig Wood, guitar, banjo	
		Henry "Den Gyldne Stemme (The Golden Voice)" Bilde, accordion, vocals	
		Vic Stewart, vocals	Town Cryers
		John Murray, guitar	Weather
		Robbie King, keys	Bobby Taylor & The Vancouvers, The Good Shepherds, Brahman, Chilliwack, Doucette, Powder Blues
		Lee Taylor, bass	Z Stamp Rock Band

BAND NAME ORIGINALLY	BAND NAMES LATER	PLAYERS [*ORIGINAL MEMBERS MARKED WITH ASTERISK WHERE KNOWN]	PLAYERS' OTHER BANDS, WHETHER EARLIER OR LATER
		Kat Hendrikse, drums	Tom Northcott & The Vancouver Playboys, Heart
		Toni Still, drums	The Living End
PH Phactor Jug Band		John Hendricks, mandolin, mandola, banjo, guitar, kazoo, jug, vocals	
		Nick Ogilvie, guitar, banjo, harp, vocals	
		John Browne, guitar, harmonica	
		Davy Coffin, guitar, mandolin	
		Chris Robinson, guitar	
		Steve Mork, bass, jug	
		Paul Bassett, drums, washboard	
		Dennis Long, drums	
		Mike Rush, drums	
Pied Pear (Pied Pumkin)		Joe Mock, guitar, piano, vocals	Joe Mock & No Commercial Potential, Mock Duck
		Shari Ulrich, fiddle, flute, vocals	Hometown Band, UHF, BTU, High Bar Gang
		Rick Scott, dulcimer, vocals	
Seeds of Time	*Rocket Norton Band, Prism*	*Bob Kripps, vocals	
		*Frank Brnjac, guitar	
		*John Hall, keys	Prism
		*Steve Walley, bass	
		*Gary "Rocket Norton" Wanstall, drums	Rocket Norton Band, Prism
		Geoff Edington, guitar, vocals	William Tell & The Marksmen
		Lindsay Mitchell, guitar	William Tell & The Marksmen, Prism
		Jerry Doucette, guitar	The Reefers, Brutus, Tribe, Abernathy Shagnaster, Homestead, Prism, Doucette
		Rick Enns, bass	Rogues, Tom Northcott Trio, United Empire Loyalists, Mock Duck
		George Greenwell, guitar, vocals	Pennywhistle, The Coastmen

BAND NAME ORIGINALLY	BAND NAMES LATER	PLAYERS [*ORIGINAL MEMBERS MARKED WITH ASTERISK WHERE KNOWN]	PLAYERS' OTHER BANDS, WHETHER EARLIER OR LATER
		Allen Hawirko (Al Harlow), bass, guitar	Segment 41, Paisley Rain, The Trees, Seeds of Time, The Burner Boys, Harlow, Prism
		Tom Lavin, guitar, vocals	Orville Dorp, Uproar, Prism, Powder Blues
		Alex Michie, sax, vocals	
Tom Northcott & The Vancouver Playboys		Tom Northcott, vocals	Tom Northcott Trio
		Ronnie Jordan, vocals	
		John Crowe, guitar	
		Dennis MacFadden, keys	
		Terry Cromie, trombone, vocals	
		Lynn Rycroft, trumpet	
		Randy Rayment, saxophone	
		Garnet Hunt, bass	
		Kat Hendrikse, drums	Papa Bear's Medicine Show, Heart
Tom Northcott Trio		Tom Northcott, guitar and vocals	Vancouver Playboys
		Rick Enns, bass, vocals	Rogues, United Empire Loyalists, Mock Duck, Seeds of Time
		Chris Dixon, drums	
United Empire Loyalists		*Anton "Tom" Kolstee, lead guitar	
		*Jeff Ridley, rhythm guitar	Uproar
		*Mike Trew, organ, vocals	
		*Bruce Dowad, bass	
		*Richard Cruickshank, drums	
		John Lome, guitar, vocals	
		Rick Enns, bass, vocals	Rogues, Tom Northcott Trio, Seeds of Time, Mock Duck
		Ted Lewis (aka Duris Maxwell), drums	The Tornadoes, The Chessmen, The Good Shepherds, Little Daddy & The Bachelors, Bobby Taylor & The Vancouvers, Privilege, Brahman, Skylark, Country Love, Heart, Doucette, Powder Blues, Johnny V; session and tour work (Eddie Money, Meatloaf, Toto)
		Glen Hendrickson, drums	Black Snake Blues Band, Mock Duck, Orville Dorp, Uproar, Shakedown

BAND NAME ORIGINALLY	BAND NAMES LATER	PLAYERS [*ORIGINAL MEMBERS MARKED WITH ASTERISK WHERE KNOWN]	PLAYERS' OTHER BANDS, WHETHER EARLIER OR LATER
The Wailers		*John Hanford, guitar, vocals	
		*John Greek, guitar	
		*Neil Rush, sax	
		*John "Buck" Ormsby, bass, vocals	
		*Ricky Lynn Johnson, drums, vocals	
		Rockin' Robin Roberts, vocals	
		Gary Favier, vocals	
		Gail Harris, vocals	
		Neil Andersson, guitar	
		Rich Dangel, guitar	
		Denny Weaver, guitar	
		Kim Eggers, sax	
		Ron Gardner, sax, vocals	
		Mark Marush, sax	
		Kent Morrill, keys, vocals	
		Jerry Werner, bass	
		Allen Lynn, drums	
		Dave Roland, drums, vocals	
		Mike Burk, drums	
William Tell & The Marksmen	*Paisley Rain*	Geoff Edington, guitar, vocals	Seeds of Time
		Lindsay Mitchell, lead guitar	Seeds of Time
		Bill Dunlaw, keys	
		Morris Hillan, bass	
		Dave Wilson, drums	
Winter's Green [aka Wintergreens, Wintergreen]		Ra McGuire, vocals	Applejack, Trooper
		Brian Smith, guitar	Applejack, Trooper
		Wayne Gibson, keys	
		Bruce Rutherford, bass	
		Stu Wilson, drums	The Family Dogs
		Derek Solbe, drums	

With thanks to webmaster Sam Carlson and the hundreds of crowdsource contributors to pnwbands.com, *a great community cultural resource since 2001.*

Selected

Discography

Bobby Taylor & The Vancouvers. *Bobby Taylor & The Vancouvers*. Tamla Motown GS930, 1968, vinyl LP (six other versions released in US, UK, Venezuela). Track listing accessed 2014-03-28 at www.discogs.com/Bobby-Taylor-And-The-Vancouvers-Bobby-Taylor-And-The-Vancouvers/release/2734247.

A1	"Does Your Mama Know About Me"	2:52
A2	"So This Is Love"	2:55
A3	"I Am Your Man"	2:58
A4	"I Heard It through the Grapevine"	2:43
A5	"Malinda"	2:52
A6	"Fading Away"	2:50
B1	"You Gave Me Something (And Everything's Alright)"	3:05
B2	"It's Growing"	2:56
B3	"One Girl"	2:25
B4	"Try a Little Tenderness"	2:52
B5	"Day by Day or Never"	2:40
B6	"If You Love Her"	2:35

Brave New World. "I See," "It's Tomorrow," "Cried," "Signed D.C.," "Fire Girl" and "Train Kept a-Rollin'" appear variously on 14 CD and LP reissue compilations listed at Discogs, accessed 2014-02-04 at www.discogs.com/artist/363194-Brave-New-World-3.

The Centaurs. "Kicks" b/w "Be Happy." Polydor Netherlands, 1967, vinyl 45. Streaming audio accessed 2014-02-04 at www.thecentaurs.com (in sidebar, click "60s Archive"). Also streaming at that page are five 1966 demos recorded at Robin Spurgin's Vancouver studio plus a previously unknown 1967 mono live recording by a fan in an Amsterdam club:

Demos

"Heart Full of Soul"

"Hungry"

"Money"

"Walk That Walk"

"Hey Little Girl"

Live mono

"Good Lovin'"

"Come On Up"

"Down The Road A Piece"

"Gimme Some Lovin'"

"Good Guys Don't Wear White"

"House of the Rising Sun"

"I Need You / Pain In My Heart"

"Mustang Sally"

"Route 66"

"CC Rider"

"Last Train to Clarksville"

"Midnight Hour"

"Money" / "Walkin' the Dog" / "Long Green"

"One More Time"

"Slowdown"

The Classics. **See** *History of Vancouver Rock and Roll, vol. 1* and The Collectors singles below.

The Collectors (Canadian releases), accessed 2014-02-04 at www.discogs.com/artist/1401570-Collectors-The-4.

Singles

as The (CFUN) Classics

"Aces High" / "Comin' Home Baby." Jaguar J2001, 1963.

"Till I Met You" / "It Didn't Take Much." Jaguar J2002, 1964.

as The Canadian Classics

"Why Don't You Love Me" / "Goodbye My Love." GNP Crescendo, 1966.

as The Collectors

"Looking at a Baby" / "Old Man." New Syndrome NS16, February 1967.

"Fisherwoman" / "Listen to the Words." New Syndrome NS20, August 1967.

"We Can Make It" / "Fat Bird." Warner Bros. 7159, January 1968.

"Lydia Purple" / "She (Will-o'-the-Wind)." New Syndrome / Warner Bros. 7194, June 1968.

"Early Morning" / "My Love Delights Me." New Syndrome / Warner Bros. 6057, June 1969.

"I Must Have Been Blind" / "Beginning Pt. 1." London M17379, January 1970.

"Sometimes We're Up" / "Beginning Pt. 2."
London M17383, April 1970.

Related releases

With Fred Latremouille of CFUN radio:
"Latromotion" / "Good Loving." London,
1964

Howie Vickers with Eternal Triangle (Tom
Northcott & Susan Jacks): "It's True" /
"Watch Me Go." New Syndrome, 1967.

Albums

The Collectors aka New Vibrations from Canada.
New Syndrome Records WS1746, 1968, vinyl LP.

Grass & Wild Strawberries. New Syndrome
Records WS1774, 1969, vinyl LP; also released as Warner Bros. WST1774C, 1969,
reel-to-reel album.

Cool Aid Benefit Album, The. Regenerator Records,
Regen 1001CD, 2010, 2-CD+DVD reissue compilation. Track listing accessed 2014-03-
28 at www.discogs.com/Various-The-Cool-
Aid-Benefit-Album/release/3156901. Deluxe,
numbered, limited-edition double LP only,
Regen1103LP, 2012, with 19 songs, mail order info and streaming 00:30 samples accessed
2014-03-28 at http://lightintheattic.net/releas-
es/578-the-cool-aid-benefit-album-deluxe-edi-
tion.

1-1.   Spring   "Bring Yourself Down to Earth
Lovin Blues, Baby"

1-2.   Mother Tucker's Yellow Duck   "I"

1-3.   Blacksnake Blues Band
"The Reason"

1-4.   Mock Duck
"Di Re Nu (false start)"

1-5.   Mock Duck   "Do Re Mi"

1-6.   Mock Duck
"Pointillistic Scherzo"

1-7.   Hydro Electric Streetcar
"Gardens and Flowers"

1-8.   Papa Bear's Medicine Show
"Golden Girl"

1-9.   Route Nine
"Girl of the Night Suite"

1-10. Nancy   "Ball in the Country"

1-11. Blacksnake Blues Band   "Catfish"

2-1.   Mock Duck   "Borrowed Song"

2-2.   Mother Tucker's Yellow Duck
"Mountain Joy"

2-3.   Hydro Electric Streetcar   "I Realize"

2-4.   Spring   "Wordplay"

2-5.   Route Nine   "Topless Lunch"

2-6.   Nancy   "No Time / Got a Feeling"

2-7.   Greydon Moore & Leo Jung
"The Planet Man"

2-8.   Blacksnake Blues Band   "Carousel"

2-9.   Hydro Electric Streetcar
"High Memory"

2-10. Mock Duck
"As the Bullet Enters Anton"

2-11. Mock Duck   "Hastings East"

2-12. *Cool Aid* album commercial jingle

3-1.   *Cool Aid* documentary

3-2.   Mock Duck   "Do Re Mi"

3-3.   Mock Duck   "Hurt on Me"

3-4.   Spring   "No Opportunity Necessary, No
Experience Needed"

3-5.   Spring   "Bring Yourself Down to Earth
Lovin Blues, Baby"

3-6.   Papa Bear's Medicine Show   "Georgie"

3-7.   Papa Bear's Medicine Show
"It's Not Over"

3-8.   Mother Tucker's Yellow Duck   "I"

3-9.   Mother Tucker's Yellow Duck
"Times Are Changin'"

History of Vancouver Rock and Roll, vol. 1. Neptoon
Records, VRCA001, 1983, vinyl LP reissue compilation. Track listing accessed 2014-03-28
at www.discogs.com/Various-The-History-
Of-Vancouver-Rock-And-Roll-Volume-1/
release/3874650.

A1   Jim Morrison [not that one]
"Ready to Rock"

A2   Les Vogt   "I'm Gonna Sit Right Down
and Cry over You"

A3   The Prowlers   "Rock Me, Baby"

A4   The Prowlers   "Get a Move On"

A5	The Canadian VIPS	"Lucille"
A6	The Stripes	"Hot Rod"
A7	Stan Cayer	"Three Wild Women"
A8	Gerry Fiander	"So Long, Goodbye"
B1	The Classics	"Aces High"
B2	The Chessmen	"Meadowlands"
B3	The Hi-Fives	"Fujikami the Warrior"
B4	The Hi-Fives	"Mean Old Woman"
B5	The Valentines	"The Sock"
B6	Les Vogt	"The Blamers"
B7	Patty Surbey	"Hey, Boy"
B8	Jim Morrison & The Stripes "Singin' the Blues"	

History of Vancouver Rock and Roll, vol. 2. Neptoon Records, VRCA002, 1985, vinyl LP reissue compilation. Track listing accessed 2014-03-28 at www.discogs.com/Various-The-History-Of-Vancouver-Rock-And-Roll-Volume-2/release/3588935.

A1	The Shockers	"Somebody Help Me"
A2	The Chessmen	"The Way You Fell"
A3	Terry Jacks	"There's No Blood in Bone"
A4	The Pacers	"I Want You Back"
A5	The Shadracks	"Call Up the Man"
A6	The Chessmen	"She Comes by Night"
A7	Fred Latremouille	"Latromotion" [**see also** under The Collectors: Related releases]
A8	Patty Surby & The Canadian VIPS "I Want a Beatle for Christmas"	
B1	The Nocturnals	"This Ain't Love"
B2	The Nocturnals	"You Lied"
B3	The Nocturnals	"Because You're Gone"
B4	Trials of Jayson Hoover	"King Size"
B5	Night Train Revue "Walk On The Wild Side"	
B6	Little Daddy & The Bachelors "Too Much Monkey Business"	
B7	Little Daddy & The Bachelors "Junior's Jerk"	

History of Vancouver Rock and Roll, vol. 3. Neptoon Records, VRCA003, 1983, vinyl LP reissue compilation. Cover art features Poster 72. Track listing accessed 2014-03-28 at www.discogs.com/Various-The-History-Of-Vancouver-Rock-And-Roll-Volume-3/release/3875239.

A1	Seeds of Time	"My Home Town" [first released as 45 b/w "Muskrat Rumble." Coast C1971, 1971]
A2	Spring (19)	"It's a New Day"
A3	Tom Northcott	"Just Don't"
A4	Painted Ship	"Little White Lies"
A5	Self Portrait	"He's a Man"
A6	United Empire Loyalists "No No No"	
A7	Winter's Green	"Are You a Monkey?"
B1	The Collectors	"Looking at a Baby"
B2	Painted Ship	"Frustration"
B3	Tom Northcott	"Let Me Know"
B4	Spring	"As Feelings Go"
B5	Northwest Company "Rock 'n' Roll Lover Man"	
B6	Seeds of Time	"Crying the Blues" [first released as 45 b/w "Baby Doll," Coast C1975, 1975]
B7	Orville Dorp	"Jesus Marijuana"

History of Vancouver Rock and Roll, vol. 4. Neptoon Records, VRCA unnumbered, 1991, CD reissue compilation. Streaming sample tracks and link to online store accessed 2014-02-04 at http://neptoonrecords.bandcamp.com/album/the-history-of-vancouver-rock-roll-volume-four.

1.	Northwest Company "Hard To Cry"	02:26
2.	Northwest Company "Get Away from It All"	02:50
3.	Northwest Company "Eight Hour Day"	01:43
4.	William Tell & The Marksmen "Mary Jane"	02:13
5.	Shockers "Love Is a Beautiful Thing"	02:41
6.	Eternal Triangle	"My New Love"	02:13

7.	Long Time Comin'	"Paper Rose"	02:40
8.	Long Time Comin' "Part of the Season"		03:14
9.	One Way Street	"Listen To Me"	01:55
10.	One Way Street	"Tears"	02:09
11.	Mock Duck	"Do Re Mi"	03:03
12.	The Look	"In a Whirl"	02:33
13.	The Collectors	"Eyes"	01:52
14.	The Collectors	"Don't Feel Bad"	02:19
15.	Silver Chalice Revue	"Soul Drifting"	02:48
16.	Spring "Country Boy Named Willy"		02:43

Little Daddy & The Bachelors. **See** *History of Vancouver Rock and Roll, vol. 2.*

Live! From the Grooveyard. Neptoon Records, Neptoon 005, 2004, CD reissue compilation. Link to online store accessed 2014-02-04 at http://neptoonrecords.bigcartel.com/product/live-from-the-grooveyard-cd. Originally released by New Syndrome Records NSLM1004, 1967, 2LP.

1.	The Epics	"It's Growing"	2:54
2.	The Epics	"Knock on Wood"	2:27
3.	Night Train Revue	"Letter Song"	2:50
4.	Night Train Revue	"99 ½"	2:31
5.	Soul Unlimited "Get Out of My Life, Woman"		2:53
6.	Soul Unlimited	"Choo Choo"	3:24
7.	Kentish Steele & The Shantelles "Have Love Will Travel"		2:34
8.	Kentish Steele & The Shantelles "Land of 1000 Dances"		3:00
9.	Kentish Steele & The Shantelles "Leaving Here"		2:14
10.	Kentish Steele & The Shantelles "Mercy Mercy"		2:45
11.	Stags	"It Won't Be Wrong"	2:12
12.	Stags	"Out of Our Tree"	3:21
13.	The Shockers	"You Don't Love Me"	2:58
14.	The Shockers	"It's You Alone"	2:52
15.	The Nocturnals	"Mustang Sally"	3:45
16.	Soul Unlimited	"Little Joe"	2:39
17.	Soul Unlimited "Something You Got"		2:40
18.	Night Train Revue "Sometimes I Wonder"		3:09
19.	Night Train Revue "You Don't Know Like I Know"		2:32
20.	The Epics	"Cleo's Back"	2:27
21.	The Epics	"If I Could Turn Back the Hands of Time"	2:04
22.	The Shockers "Don't Bring Me Down"		3:08
23.	The Shockers	"You Better Run"	2:16
24.	The Nocturnals	"Slow Down"	2:56
25.	The Nocturnals "You Make Me Feel So Good"		3:17
26.	The Nocturnals	"Get On Back"	2:43
27.	The Stags	"Drive My Car"	2:20
28.	The Stags "Everybody Knows (I Still Love You)"		1:50

Liverpool Five. Full details accessed 2014-04-14 at www.discogs.com/artist/847531-Liverpool-Five.

Singles

"Tokio" / "Skinny Minny," CBS CBS1623, 1964, vinyl 45.

"If You Gotta Go, Go Now" / "Too Far Out," RCA Victor, 1965, vinyl 45.

"Everything's Alright" / "That's What I Want," RCA Victor, 1965, vinyl 45.

"New Directions" / "What a Crazy World (We're Living In)," RCA Victor, 1966, vinyl 45.

"Any Way You Want Me" / "The Snake," RCA Victor, 1966, vinyl 45.

"Heart" / "I Just Can't Believe It," RCA Victor, 1965, vinyl 45.

"She's Mine" / "Heart," Victor SS1733, 1966, vinyl 45.

"She's Mine" / "Sister Love" (promo single), RCA Victor 47-8816, 1966, vinyl 45.

"Cloudy" / "She's (Got Plenty of Love)" (promo single), RCA Victor 47-9158, 1967, vinyl 45.

Albums

Tokio International, CBS, 1965, vinyl LP.

Arrive, RCA Victor, 1966, vinyl LP.

Out of Sight, RCA Victor, 1967, vinyl LP.

Compilations

The Astronauts / Liverpool Five, RCA Victor PRS-251, 1967, vinyl LP.

Mack, Danny. Complete album discography appears at the artist's website, accessed 2014-04-04 at www.dannymack.com/index.php/albums.

Mock Duck. *Test Record*. Gear Fab Records, GF154, 2000, CD reissue. Mail order info accessed 2014-02-04 at http://gearfab.swiftsite.com/Catalog_List/Catalog_List/catalog_39a.html. Streaming sample tracks accessed 2014-02-04 at www.allmusic.com/album/test-record-mw0000069461. Original title was a limited-release acetate pressing of tracks 1–5 recorded live at Village Bistro, Vancouver, 1968, plus two other tracks. Four additional tracks were released as singles, also in 1968.

1.	"Home Made Jam/Introduction"	12:43
2.	"Ground Hog"	4:58
3.	"Hurt on Me"	2:47
4.	"Sitting on Top of the World"	4:14
5.	"My Time"	6:39
6.	"Fat Man"	4:49
7.	"Crosscut Saw"	3:45
8.	"Easter Dog"	2:54
9.	"Funky Song"	4:43
10.	"Do Re Mi"	3:02
11.	"Playing Games"	3:04
12.	"Jazz Mock"	19:48

Night Train Revue. **See** *History of Vancouver Rock and Roll, vol. 2* and *Live! From the Grooveyard*.

Nocturnals, The. *Greatest Hits & More!* Neptoon Records, Neptoon 010, 2006, CD reissue (15 tracks) plus DVD (55:00, NTSC all regions), 2007. Mail order info and links to streaming sample tracks accessed 2014-02-04 at http://neptoonrecords.bigcartel.com/product/the-nocturnals-greatest-hits-and-more-cd-dvd. **See also** *History of Vancouver Rock and Roll, vol. 2* and *Live! From the Grooveyard*.

1.	"This Ain't Love"	03:20
2.	"Because You're Gone"	02:24

3.	"Lovin' Blues"	02:49
4.	"You Lied"	02:18
5.	"Detroit"	02:55
6.	"I Don't Love Her No More"	01:58
7.	"Uptown"	03:10
8.	"Can It Be True"	02:16
9.	"Do What You Want"	03:09
10.	"I Found a Love"	02:41
11.	"Why?"	02:31
12.	"Look Around You"	02:31
13.	"Ain't No Big Thing"	03:08
14.	"I'll Walk Away"	02:11
15.	"I Don't Love Her No More" (alternative version)	02:05

Northcott, Tom. Listing compiled from Discogs, accessed 2014-04-14 at www.discogs.com/artist/725489-Tom-Northcott.

Singles

"Cry Tomorrow" / "She Loves Me, She Loves Me Not." Syndrome Records, 1-1001/2, 1965, vinyl 45 (as Tom Northcott & The Vancouver Playboys).

"Crazy Jane" / "The Collector." New Syndrome Records, NS-106, 1969, vinyl 45.

"Suzanne" / "Spaceship Races." UNI Records, UNI55282, 1971, vinyl 45.

"I Think It's Going To Rain Today" / "It's True." UNI Records, UNI55267, 1971, vinyl 45.

"Other Times" / "1941." Warner Bros., 7160, n.d., promotional vinyl 45 (prod. Lenny Waronker, Leon Russell; arr. Leon Russell).

Album

Upside, Downside. UNI Records, UNI73108, 1971, vinyl LP.

Compilations

The Best of Tom Northcott 1964 to 1971. Neptoon Records, Neptoon003, n.d., vinyl LP compilation.

Sunny Goodge Street: The Warner Bros. Recordings. Rhino Handmade RHM2-524879 (US), 2012, CD compilation, limited edition with letterpress-printed folio designed by Bruce Licher featuring psychedelic illustration by Bob Masse.

Northwest Company. *The Northwest Company 1966–1973: Eight-Hour Day*. Neptoon Records, 2003, CD reissue. Mail order info and links to streaming sample tracks accessed 2014-02-04 at http://neptoonrecords.bigcartel.com/product/the-northwest-company-1966-1976-eight-hour-day-cd. **See also** *History of Vancouver Rock and Roll, vol. 3* and *vol. 4*.

1.	"Get Away From It All"	02:49
2.	"Hard To Cry"	02:24
3.	"Eight Hour Day"	01:42
4.	"The End Is Autumn"	02:07
5.	"She's a Woman	03:14
6.	"Time for Everyone"	02:08
7.	"Can You Remember"	03:00
8.	"The Sunday Song"	01:49
9.	"Rock 'n' Roll Lover Man"	02:57
10.	"Let It All"	04:44
11.	"(Everybody's Got To) Care"	03:24
12.	"Don't Hear Me Complain"	02:23
13.	"Sweet Suzie"	02:56
14.	"Ain't Nothin' Wrong with Rock 'n' Roll"	04:21
15.	"Moma Moma" (live)	03:18
16.	"Grey Skies" (live)	05:48
17.	"Be Bop Baby' (live)	05:22
18.	"Policeman's Coming" (live)	10:30
19.	"Hard To Cry" (demo)	02:08
20.	"Each Day" (demo)	02:06
21.	"Get Away From It All" (demo)	02:42
22.	"Ballad of a Tragic Fat Man" (demo)	02:40

Painted Ship. Accessed 2014-02-04 at www.discogs.com/artist/262554-Painted-Ship-The. **See also** *History of Vancouver Rock and Roll, vol. 3*.

"Audience Reflections" / "And She Said Yes." London Records M17354, 1966, vinyl 45.

"Frustration" / "I Told Little White Lies." London Records M17351, 1967, vinyl 45; also released 1967 in US as Mercury 72662 and in UK as Mercury MF988.

PH Phactor Jug Band. "Barefoot John" / "Minglewood Blues." Piccadilly Records 241 (US), 1967, vinyl 45.

Seeds of Time. **See** *History of Vancouver Rock and Roll, vol. 3*.

United Empire Loyalists. **See also** *History of Vancouver Rock and Roll, vol. 3*.

Single

"No, No, No" / "Afraid of the Dark." [Private label] CT-35707-08, 1968, limited-release vinyl 45.

Albums

Notes from the Underground. N.p., PNCD1214, 1998, reissue CD. Tracks which are also included on the Nasoni Records release listed just below are omitted from the contents list for this album, accessed 2014-04-14 at the Museum of Canadian Music, www.mocm.ca/Music/Title.aspx?TitleId=305292:

"Hangin' Around"

"I Know You Rider"

"It's Alright"

"Tired Eyes"

"My Chances for Living"

United Empire Loyalists. Nasoni Records (Germany), Nasoni 010, 2000, vinyl LP.

A1	"No, No, No"
A2	"Afraid of the Dark"
A3	"Otis"
A4	"Buffalo Wilkie"
A5	"Columbus"
B1	"Lookin' and Searchin'"
B2	"Wait a Minute Jim"
B3	"Different Drummer"
B4	"Look Who We Are"
B5	"You Don't Love Me"

Vogt, Les. "The Blamers" / "Moon Rocketin." Apt Records/ABC Paramount, 45-25042, Apt 45-1508, 1960, vinyl 45. **See also** *History of Vancouver Rock and Roll, vol. 1.*

William Tell & The Marksmen. **See** *History of Vancouver Rock and Roll, vol. 4.*

Winter's Green. **See** *History of Vancouver Rock and Roll, vol. 3.*

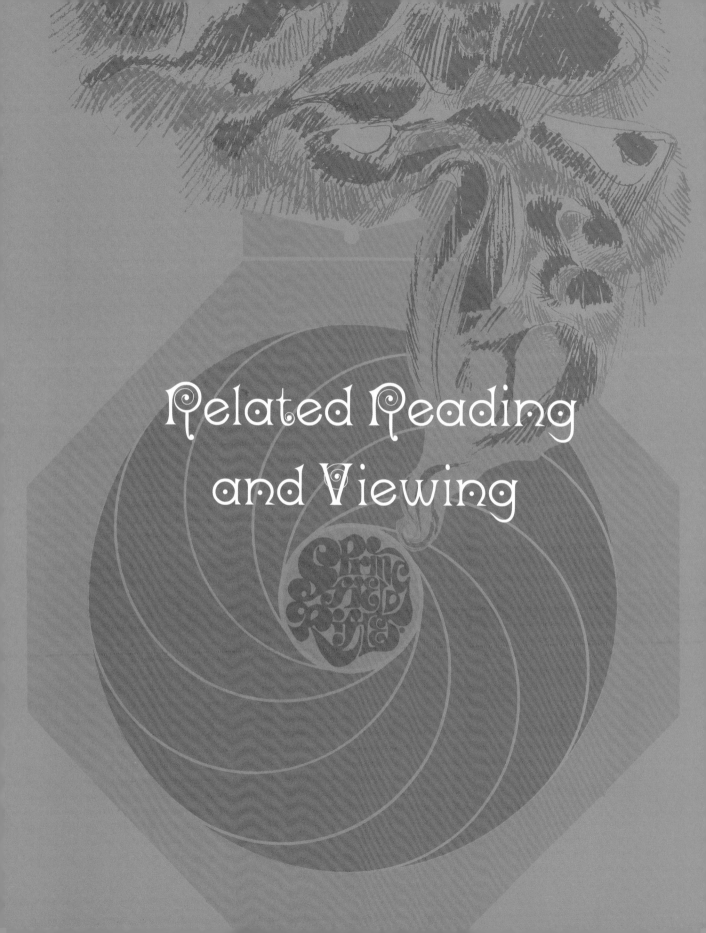

Related Reading and Viewing

"About Red." *Red Robinson: Rockin' Radio for 60 Years* (blog). Accessed 2014-05-04 at http://red-robinson.com/blog/?page_id=2.

Aicher, Bill. "Musician, Club-owner, Manager; What *Can't* Gary Taylor Do?" *Music Critic* (website), Apr. 2000. Accessed 2014-03-28 at www.music-critic.com/interviews/garytaylor.htm.

a/k/a Tommy Chong: United States of America v. Thomas B Kin Chong. A Josh Gilbert documentary featuring Tommy Chong, Cheech Marin, Shelby Chong, Lou Adler and Paris Chong. Santa Monica, Calif.: Blue Chief Entertainment Inc., Awesome Documentaries LLC, 2008. DVD (NTSC, 1:20:00). Trailer accessed 2014-05-01 at www.akatommychong.com/media.html.

Aronsen, Lawrence. *City of Love and Revolution: Vancouver in the Sixties*. Vancouver: New Star Books, 2010.

Batten, Jack. "Vancouver: How the Town's Fighting the Dread Hippie Menace." *Maclean's* (Aug. 1967): 18.

Blecha, Peter. "Pat O'Day, Godfather of Northwest Rock?" HistoryLink.org essay 3130, Apr. 3, 2001. Accessed 2014-03-28 at http://is.gd/FhaWaC.

CBC TV. "Hippie Life: It Ain't Easy." CBC TV Digital Archives videoclip (6:43). Accessed 2014-03-28 at www.cbc.ca/archives/categories/society/youth/hippie-society-the-youth-rebellion/hippie-life-it-aint-easy.html.

———. "Hippie Youth: Vancouver's Human Be-in, Mar. 26, 1967, at Ceperley Meadow in Stanley Park." CBC TV Digital Archives videoclip (14:45). Accessed 2014-03-28 at www.cbc.ca/archives/categories/society/youth/hippie-society-the-youth-rebellion/festivals-and-happenings-vancouvers-human-be-in.html.

———. "Vancouver Politician Averse to Hippies: Mayor Defends the Recent Arrest of Several Youths Caught Loitering, Calling the Hippies 'Parasites' and 'Scum,'" Mar. 18, 1968. CBC TV Digital Archives videoclip (6:46). Accessed 2014-03-28 at www.cbc.ca/player/Digital+Archives/Society/Youth/ID/1788978410/?page=5.

Chong, Thomas. *The I Chong: Meditations from the Joint*. New York: Simon Spotlight Entertainment, 2006.

———. "Tommy Chong's Vancouver." *Cannabis Culture* 68 (Fall 2007), posted to web Aug. 24, 2008. Accessed 2014-03-28 at www.cannabisculture.com/node/10144.

Cleanliness and Godliness Skiffle Band. Webpage family tree created by Ross Hannan and Corry Arnold, 2004–2013, tracing the musical origins of Country Joe & The Fish from their earliest days in the Instant Action Jug Band, Berkeley. Accessed 2014-08-20 at www.chickenonaunicycle.com/Cleanliness and Godliness.htm.

Davis, Chuck. *The Chuck Davis History of Metropolitan Vancouver*. Vancouver: Harbour Publishing, 2011.

Davis, Chuck, et al. *The History of Metropolitan Vancouver*. Website developed and administered by Quasar Design & Data Management Inc., 2004–2011. Chronology for 1967 at "May 5" re Dan McLeod and the *Georgia Straight*. Accessed 2014-05-01 at www.vancouverhistory.ca/chronology1967.htm.

Donahue, Tom. "AM Radio: Stinking Up the Airwaves." *Rolling Stone* (Nov. 23, 1967): 14–15. Reprinted in *The Rock History Reader*, edited by Theo Cateforis, 103–105. New York: Routledge, 2007. Google Books excerpt accessed 2014-03-28 at http://is.gd/wgfq2x.

Donaldson, Jesse. "'It's a Filthy, Perverted Paper': A History of the *Georgia Straight*." *The Dependent Magazine*, Jul. 13, 2010. Accessed 2014-03-28 at http://thedependent.ca/featured/"it's-a-filthy-perverted-paper"-a-history-of-the-georgia-straight.

Edwardson, Ryan. *Canuck Rock: A History of Canadian Popular Music*. Toronto: University of Toronto Press, 2009.

F., Anders. "Interview with William Hay (Painted Ship)." *Klissete Fingers* (blog), posted Mar. 18, 2013. Accessed 2014-03-28 at http://yourstickyfingers.blogspot.ca/2013/03/interview-william-haythe-painted-ship.html.

Gawle, Darren. "United Empire Loyalists." *Mongrel Zine* 11 (Apr. 2013): 1–8. Accessed 2014-03-28 (HTML and page scans) at www.mongrelzine.ca/blog/united-empire-loyalists.

———. "United Empire Loyalists: Interviews with Jeff Ridley, Rick Enns and Richard Cruickshank." Webpage, Jul. 2000. Accessed 2014-03-28 at http://armenia.city.tripod.com/UEL/UEL.htm.

"Grateful Dead First Free Concert: Aug. 5, 1966, English Bay Beach Bandstand, Vancouver, BC." *Lost Live Dead* (blog), posted Dec. 24, 2009, by Corry342. Accessed 2014-03-28 at http://lostlivedead.blogspot.ca/2009/12/august-5-1966-english-bay-beach.html.

"Grateful Dead Interview." *Mojo-Navigator R&R News* 4 (Aug. 30, 1966): 1–6. Accessed 2014-03-28 (pdf) from www.rockmine.com/Archive/Library/Mojo.html.

Grushkin, Paul. *The Art of Rock: Posters from Presley to Punk.* New York: Abbeville Press, 1987.

Grushkin, Paul, and Dennis King. *Art of Modern Rock: The Poster Explosion.* San Francisco: Chronicle Books, 2004.

Grushkin, Paul, and Rob Roth. *The Art of Classic Rock.* New York: Collins Design, 2010.

Heilman, Jaymie. "Offspring as Enemy? How Canada's National Magazine Confronted Youth and Youth Culture in the 1960s." *Past Imperfect* 6 (1997): 73–110. Accessed 2014-03-28 (pdf) at http://ejournals.library.ualberta.ca/index.php/pi/article/viewFile/1424/965.

Jordan, Janelle. "War on Drugs a Global Failure, London School of Economics Says." CBC News, May 9, 2014. Accessed 2014-05-01 at http://is.gd/VlBVvP.

Kluckner, Michael. *Vancouver Remembered.* North Vancouver: Whitecap Books, 2006.

Kostash, Myrna. *Long Way from Home: The Story of the Sixties Generation in Canada.* Toronto: Lorimer, 1980.

Loo, Tina. "Flower Children in Lotusland." *Beaver* 7, no. 1 (Feb./Mar. 1998): 36–42. EBSCOhost Academic Search Premier, doc. 274328. Accessed 2014-03-28 via proxy server (consult your local public library).

Mackie, John. "When Vinyl Was King: Collectors Harvest Rare '60s Discs from Vancouver's Rock 'n' Roll Infancy." *Vancouver Sun*, Nov. 26, 2010, reprinted (pdf) at the Museum of Canadian Music. Accessed 2014-04-14 at www.mocm.ca/Home.aspx (linked from "Media Clippings" section at bottom of webpage).

Martel, Marcel. "'They Smell Bad, Have Diseases and Are Lazy': RCMP Officers Reporting on Hippies in the Late Sixties." *Canadian Historical Review* 90, no. 2 (2009): 215–245. EBSCOhost Academic Search Premier, doc. 40634552. Accessed 2014-03-28 (pdf) via proxy server (consult your local public library).

Norton, Rocket. *Rocket Norton: Lost in Space.* Vancouver: Amazing Books, 2006.

Owram, Doug. *Born at the Right Time: A History of the Baby-Boom Generation.* Toronto: University of Toronto Press, 1996.

Pauls, Naomi, and Charles Campbell. *The Georgia Straight: What the Hell Happened?* Vancouver: Douglas & McIntyre, 1997.

Pettipas, Keith. "United Empire Loyalists: *Notes from the Underground.*" Profile of the band and interview with guitarist Jeff Ridley. Museum of Canadian Music, accessed 2014-04-14 at www.mocm.ca/Music/Title.aspx?TitleId=305292.

Ross, Daniel. "Panic on Love Street: Citizens and Local Government Respond to Vancouver's Hippie Problem, 1967–68." *BC Studies* 180 (Winter 2013/2014): 11–41. EBSCOhost Canadian Reference Centre, doc. 94272157. Accessed 2014-03-28 (pdf) via proxy server (consult your local public library).

Ruins in Process: Vancouver Art in the Sixties. Website edited by Glenn Alteen, Lorna Brown and Scott Watson. Vancouver: Morris and Helen Belkin Art Gallery at UBC and grunt gallery, n.d. Cross-linked tables of titles (by year) and people (alphabetical) accessed 2014-04-04 at http://vancouverartinthesixties.com/archive.

Schwartz, Daniel. "Marijuana Was Criminalized in 1923, But Why?" CBC News | Health, May 3, 2014. Accessed 2014-05-04 at http://is.gd/h6IACQ.

Simpson, Gregg. "Motion Studio." *The Sound Gallery, Motion Studio and Intermedia* (blog), posted Dec. 30, 2010. Accessed 2014-03-28 at http://soundgalleryintermedia.blogspot.ca/2010/12/motion-studio.html.

———. "The Sound Gallery: The Official History of the Sound Gallery/Motion Studio and Chronology of Intermedia 1967–1973." *GreggSimpson.com*, 2012. Accessed 2014-03-28 at www.greggsimpson.com/soundgallerymotionstudio.htm.

Szatmary, David P. *Rockin' in Time: A Social History of Rock and Roll.* 7th ed. Upper Saddle River, NJ: Prentice Hall, 2010.

Verzuh, Ron. *Underground Times: Canada's Flower-Child Revolutionaries.* Toronto: Deneau, 1989.

Watson, Dave. "Vancouver Easter Be-In." *Georgia Straight*, May 8, 1997. Reprinted at the wiki "A Band Is a Beautiful Thing: The Story of the Rise and Fall of the Great Vancouver Rock Band The Burner Boys." Accessed 2014-03-28 at http://burnerboys.pbworks.com/w/page/11207088/Easter Be-In.

"'Where It's At' TV show, Vancouver, BC, late 1960s." *Rock Archaeology 101* (blog), posted Nov. 29, 2009, by Corry342. Accessed 2014-07-15 at http://rockarchaeology101.blogspot.ca/2009/11/where-its-at-tv-show-vancouver-bc-late.html.

Yorke, Ritchie. *Axes, Chops & Hot Licks: The Canadian Rock Music Scene.* Edmonton: M.G. Hurtig, 1971.

Index of Names

ORDERS

If you would like to order any of the posters featured in this book please contact Afterthought Enterprises via email:

sales@afterthoughtbook.com

Copyright © 2014 Jerry Kruz

All rights reserved. No part of this publication may be reproduced, stored in a retrieval system, or transmitted in any form or by any means—electronic, mechanical, audio recording, or otherwise—without the written permission of the publisher or a photocopying licence from Access Copyright, Toronto, Canada.

Rocky Mountain Books
www.rmbooks.com

Library and Archives Canada Cataloguing in Publication

Kruz, Jerry, 1948-, author
The afterthought : west coast rock posters and recollections from the '60s / Jerry Kruz.

Includes bibliographical references.
Issued in print and electronic formats.

ISBN 978-1-77160-024-8 (bound).—ISBN 978-1-77160-025-5 (html).—ISBN 978-1-77160-026-2 (pbf)

1. Rock music—Posters. 2. Rock musicians—Posters. 3. Rock groups—Posters.
4. Rock music—1961-1970—Discography. 5. Rock musicians—Biography.
6. Rock groups—Biography. 7. Posters—British Columbia—History. I. Title.

ML3534.K78 2014   781.66022'2   C2014-904011-3
C2014-904012-1

Printed in Canada

Rocky Mountain Books acknowledges the financial support for its publishing program from the Government of Canada through the Canada Book Fund (CBF) and the Canada Council for the Arts, and from the province of British Columbia through the British Columbia Arts Council and the Book Publishing Tax Credit.

 Canadian Heritage   Patrimoine canadien
 Canada Council for the Arts   Conseil des Arts du Canada
 BRITISH COLUMBIA ARTS COUNCIL
Supported by the Province of British Columbia

This book was produced using FSC®-certified, acid-free paper, processed chlorine free and printed with vegetable-based inks.